D1474583

More Aster(ix) Anthologies

Winter Fiction
December 2021

Best of Hot Metal Bridge
April 2021

The Ferrante Project
October 2020

The Poetry Issue
Winter 2020

Inheritance
Summer 2019

(Un)bound [double issue]
Winter 2018/2019

as well as...

Edges - Fall 2018

Dirty Laundry - Fall 2017

Kitchen Table Translation - Summer 2017

Best of Kweli - Spring 2017

What We Love - Fall 2016

and more!

available for order wherever books are sold

and don't forget to visit
asterixjournal.com
for more content and information

Aster(ix) Journal
www.asterixjournal.com

Editor-in-Chief/Founder
Angie Cruz

Publisher/Founder
Adriana E. Ramírez

Managing Editor
Amanda Tien

Contributing Editors for
Mothers Unearthed
Francesca Caccamo
Amaris Castillo
Natalia Figueroa Barroso
Bianca Hernandez
Cory Holding
Clarissa A. León
Dr. Lorna Perez
Kiera O'Brien
Blanca Torres

Aster(ix) Contributing Editors
Rosa Alcalá, Arielle
Greenberg, Yona Harvey,
Daisy Hernandez, J. A. Howard,
Sheila Maldonado, Dawn
Lundy Martin, Oindrila
Mukherjee, Idra Novey,
Emily Raboteau, Nelly Rosario,
Zohra Saed, Sun Yung Shin,
Jenelle Troxell, Chika Unigwe,
Marta Lucía Vargas, Autumn
Womack, Elleni Centime Zeleke

Advisory Editors
Ari Ariel, Armando Garcia,
Amy Sara Carroll, Norma
Cantú, Xochi Candalaria,
Jennifer Clement, Edwidge
Danticat, Cristina García,
Stephanie Elizondo Griest,
Andrea Thome, Helena Maria
Viramontes

Aster(ix) print issues are usually published twice a year with additional content online. **Aster(ix)** is funded in part by the Dietrich School of Arts and Sciences and the Department of English at University of Pittsburgh.

Aster(ix) Journal

presents

Mothers Unearthed

.✳ .✳ .✳

Edited by
Emily Raboteau & Tanya Shirazi

September 2022

BLUE SKETCH PRESS | PITTSBURGH

ASTER(IX)—Mothers Unearthed: September 2022.
Copyright © 2022 by Aster(ix) Journal.

Individual acknowledgments available on pg. 195

Published via Blue Sketch Press, Pittsburgh.
www.bluesketchpress.com

Mothers Unearthed: September 2022
An Aster(ix) Anthology / Aster(ix) Journal
Edited by Emily Raboteau & Tanya Shirazi—1st ed.

ISBN (print)   978-1-942547-18-1 (trade paperback)
                  1-942547-18-1 (ISBN-10)

Cover art by Jessica Bethel
Cover Design by Little Owl Creative

First Edition: September 2022

Printed in the United States of America
9 8 7 6 5 4 3 2 1

Contents

A CONVERSATION BETWEEN THE EDITORS

Emily Raboteau & Tanya Shirazi

Emily Raboteau: This issue of *Aster(ix)* came about in tandem with a folio I edited for the *Kenyon Review*, called "Angry Mamas." I wanted to make a space in that publication for writers to express anger about the climate crisis from the perspective of motherhood. I myself have been increasingly writing from this standpoint, because it feels urgent. I solicited many writers I admire to contribute. So many women submitted work that there was not enough space to include all of their contributions in that frame, despite the work being generally excellent and timely. How could I, in good faith, reject urgent and excellent work? I complained of this problem to Angie Cruz, *Aster(ix)*'s co-founder, who made me see it as a good problem. Look how many writers have something to say about this! Her solution was to publish all the work that could not fit into the *Kenyon Review* folio into a companion issue of *Aster(ix)*. This *Mothers Unearthed* issue is therefore a sister of and in conversation with the "Angry Mamas" folio in the *Kenyon Review*, coming out around the same time in the summer of 2022. Having curated the works in this volume, I am grateful to Tanya Shirazi, who stepped in to do the heavy labor of editing the collection. Tanya, what did you notice in your role as editor that holds these unique pieces together to make a whole?

Tanya Shirazi: It was such a joy to work on this issue, Emily. The works in *Mothers Unearthed* show how mothers re-experience and witness environmental (and social) catastrophe. They excavate and reinscribe the meaning of protectors as mothers. The fear, anger and cautionary hope is palpable in each of the pieces. Each work shows how these different crises impact their children. It's horrific to contend with what kind of world our children will inherit, what we leave behind. The mismanagement of the COVID pandemic pulses quietly throughout several of these works, as a reminder that we've already been marked in a way that makes it impossible for any of us to look away, to ignore. In what ways do you feel the perspective of motherhood has layered the work?

ER: Well, I think it allowed some of the writers to be messy, emotional, experimental, and engaged on a heart level instead of a purely analytical or data-driven level. What about you? Obviously, there are a few different genres reflected here. Not just nonfiction, which is my wheelhouse.

TS: What drew me the most to these pieces were how the children were the loudest and most honest archivists of our times. There's so much care and catharsis on the page. The title *Mothers Unearthed* perfectly sums up the movement of the pieces: they're urgent, require an intense amount of excavation, and provoke the readers so keep digging. Writing from the point of view of a mother must be so tricky. Our kids are so attached to who we are, and the way they process the world deeply affects us. I think it's that honest fear that adds so much momentum and care to the pieces. There's an immediate need to care, we can be persuaded by data and statistics that show us our climate crisis is dire, it's already here. Our government has failed us when managing a global pandemic, the numbers are our evidence. But it's terrifying knowing our children are impacted by these choices. There's comfort knowing that our actions can still have some positive consequences. Like Claire Boyle States in "Making Our Own Weather", "we are, all of us, already making our own weather, and we have choices, and there is still time." The fiction pieces... Deesha Philyaw's "Concerning the Sea Stars" and Chika Unigwe's "Water" contending with the hardships of motherhood with unreliable partners, to the hilarious and dark narration of "The Recycling at Isaiah Gardens" and the lucklaster attempt to control tenant behavior to more desirable practices. It's some dark, funny, honest work.

ER: Yes, I appreciated the humor in Carolyn Ferrell's story that you just referenced, and some of the other pieces, since humor is one of our best survival mechanisms given the compound crises our children are inheriting. Gardening is another. That's why I really loved Vanessa Martir's essay, "Dreaming a Sacred Garden." It was important to me to solicit work predominantly from women of color whose traditions and legacies of historical survival allow for registers beyond anxiety. When your ancestors have survived enslavement, for example, Jim Crow, incarceration, internment, civil war, or other seemingly insurmountable odds, the climate crisis does not appear to be the first existential threat.

TS: Deesha Philyaw's "Concerning the Sea Stars" has some really dark humorous moments around parenting and uses social media to showcase the fallout of a romantic relationship. Kianny Antigua's "She Doesn't Want to Be Called a Human" is unflinching in involving her seven-year-old Mía's perspective. The use of her daughter's poetry, drawings and her little idioms make a great point in showing us who's to blame for our demise: ourselves! Mía's right, "humans suck!" Nimmi Gowrinathan's "Unconscious" son's question, when he realizes the climate crisis will be responsible for the extinction of marine life,

"How will my grandchildren fish?" made me laugh at his foresight of caring for his non-existent children, but also drew some shame out of me, for sure.

Yes, I think that the selection of women writers of color has allowed for the curation of pieces that already show inherited injustices you've mentioned and compounded with immediate loss. From forest to wildfires, lives to the COVID-19 pandemic, our sense of safety in the face of social injustice, climate crisis, and public health. It's very personal, and all on these pages.

Mothers Unearthed is here, go read!

Climate Refuge

Sujatha Fernandes

When Hurricane Irene pummels upstate New York in the summer of 2011, we are there on vacation. My father-in-law wakes us at 6am after the creek by our rental house overflows. My husband and I strap our children, aged two years and five months, into our car under gale force winds and we drive across a flooding river to get away.

Hurricane Sandy hit us at home in New York City just fourteen months later, the largest hurricane ever in the mid-Atlantic and Northeast region. In the first few years of their lives, my children lived through two of the worst storms in East Coast history.

As the polar ice caps melt and the planet warms, extreme weather events hit with more severity and greater frequency. There are monster hurricanes, tsunamis, earthquakes, wildfires, and floods. Myself and other mamas wonder, how can we keep our children safe in the face of worsening climate disasters? Where can we find a climate refuge?

Being a mother ignites some dormant, powerful feeling within me to shelter my children from harm. Maybe it is experiencing for the first time another being who is completely dependent on you for their survival. Maybe it is the knowledge that their tiny bodies, unformed infant skulls, wobbly heads are so vulnerable to injury. Maybe it is the feeling of responsibility for bringing them into this beautiful, chaotic, terrifying world. I have never believed in the instincts of motherhood as biological; that would deny the mothers who do not feel this way. I can't explain my own reactions. I surprise myself the day my toddler son runs onto the road and I pull him back with such force that I fall and injure my hand. My desire to protect him is more than the fear of bodily harm to myself.

My close friend Devi, a Narungga Kaurna woman back home in Australia dreams of taking her two girls out to live on country, where they could learn to forage, fish, and grow their own food like her ancestors. When food production and supply chains are disrupted by climate change, she says, we'll have to go back to the old ways.

I dream of raising my children in my coastal South Indian hometown of Mangalore. I have childhood memories of chasing roosters in the yard of my father's ancestral house, drinking juice from the tender green coconuts of our tree. In my mother's ancestral place in neighboring Udipi, her family cultivated rice fields behind the house. I roamed with my cousins through the fields, watching while the harvested paddy was threshed. There is a photo of me at age two with my cousin Saritha in front of the mighty kasalo plant, its leaves twice my size.

But Mangalore has changed. The region has been prey to the mining industry and transformed by overzealous developers. The lime green paddy fields, lush mangroves, and red dirt roads of my ancestral home have been replaced by shiny new hotels, mall complexes, and luxury apartments. Mangalore, like most of the country, has PM levels higher than what is considered safe to inhale. Children in India have greater levels of asthma and decreased lung function, and are more prone to cognitive impairment.

We decide to move to Sydney: my American husband, my two kids, and myself. My LA-based friend Priya has taken her boys and moved back to Melbourne. If we live away from the coasts and the bush, we might be safe from floods and fires. Another friend Yadira, an Afro Puerto Rican woman from the Bronx, has also moved with her husband and two children to Melbourne. She is after another kind of refuge, from gun violence against Black people, though she knows they are still not safe from racism and injustice.

I want to be near my parents and my large extended family. In Sydney, we can raise our children close to nature, with national parks and hiking trails nearby.

The Domain, Gadigal land, September 2019

The younger generation is mobilizing for climate justice. School children around Australia are organizing climate strikes as part of a global wave of protests. I pick up my son S from school and take him to the Global Climate Strike on the grassy lawns of The Domain in downtown Sydney, on the unceded lands of the Gadigal people. S is thrilled to protest. He has made a sign that says, "Why do we need more buildings?" In the few years since we moved to Sydney, S has seen new developments go up on all sides of us.

I text my mama friends to see who is coming. On the street we bump into Justine and her son. The kids play word games on the train. Sonja is stuck at work. Susan sends me a photo of her and her daughter with their signs at the university; they are marching from there to The Domain with a contingent from the union. We make plans to meet up, but when we arrive to the 80,000 strong protest, we have no chance of finding each other. All around me are school children with ponytails, kids carried in their parents' arms. S holds his sign up proudly. A curly haired little girl with the Extinction Rebellion symbol on her forehead carries a placard that says, "It's Not Us. It's You! 100 companies = 71% emissions."

The protest opens with a Welcome to Country from Aunty Rhonda Dixon-Grovenor, a Darug Yuin elder. "We stand together, my brothers and sisters," she says. "We send a message all around the world, we're united together. We stand as brothers and sisters to fight for the right of Mother Earth, and our waters, our riverways." The crowd roars.

Aunty Rhonda introduces Gadrian Hoosan, a Garrwa Yanyuwa man from Borroloola, a remote community in the Gulf of Carpentaria. The rhythmic chants of his fiery voice with clapping sticks, and the black, red, and yellow Aboriginal flags across the stage and in the audience, remind us that this is an ancient land. Hoosan tells us that in his remote community in the Northern Territory, they can't drink the water because mining companies, supported by the government, have destroyed their water sources. This has been going on since colonization. But he has survived. He has journeyed three days to tell us that.

"We are all one family," says Hoosan, to massive cheers from the audience. "Black and white. A climate justice family."

Their words make me wonder whether, in a time of climate emergency, as a mother, I have narrowed my energies to my own children. Finding a refuge for them. I am part of a privileged minority of mamas who can even make these choices. My friend Arlene in Texas has her son in the Texas prison system. She fears if a monstrous hurricane were to damage the prison, he could be reclassified and housed far away from her.

The Aboriginal speakers are talking about kin as all people, as all life on earth, as Mother Earth itself. That care should be extended from my own children to encompass all children and life on the planet, as mutually dependent for survival.

The event is organized and led by school children. We hear their stories, their concerns, their anger. "The number one cause of this crisis," says fifteen year old student Daisy Jeffery, "is the mining and burning of coal, oil, and gas." The government should be transitioning us to clean energy sources, she goes on, but instead they are helping billionaire companies like Adani that are trashing our environment and have removed the Wangan and Jagalingou people from their own land in the Galilee Basin to turn it into a mega-mine.

The school climate strikes in Australia the previous November were the largest school strikes in the world. It's not surprising given that the continent is at elevated risk from climate change. The number of record hot days has doubled since the 1950s. Heatwaves are longer and hotter, leading to unprecedented bushfires. Weather charts now have added categories to indicate over 50 degrees Celsius (122 Fahrenheit). the fire-danger rating system has a new "Catastrophic" level. Flooding, droughts, and cyclones have become deadly. And yet, Australia has been the world's largest exporter of coal for most of the twenty-first century. In 2012, the government proposed nine new coal mines in the Galilee Basin of Central Queensland, five of which would be the biggest coal mines in the world.

My throat tightens and my eyes fill with tears as I stand with and for my son and our climate justice family on Gadigal land. There is a text from Sonja. She has picked up her sons from school and is on her way to the protest.

MOTHERS UNEARTHED

Blue Mountains, Darug and Gundungurra land, October 2019
One of our favorite hikes in Sydney is the Grand Canyon trail in the Blue Mountains. It starts from a lookout where you can see views of the sweeping valley below. Forested hills rise in peaks where they meet sandstone walls topped by grassy plateaus.

Eleven-year-old A leads the way down the steep descent of the trail, binoculars in hand. During our hikes, she has spotted kookaburras, cockatoos, and a satin bowerbird. S, eight-years-old, is cautious. He and I walk together, slower than the others.

All around us is bushland: towering eucalyptus trees with papery bark and the mottled trunks of spotted gums. Dry leaves crunch underfoot and we notice how parched the land is. Sydney has been experiencing drought for the past year, and the region has gone for a long time without much rainfall.

Further below, the trail passes through rainforest. Water splashes down from waterfalls. Giant ferns grow along the sides of the path. The abundant roots of the coachwood trees are covered in moss. We cross over the creeks by skipping from one stone to the next.

The climb back up is almost vertical and I stop to catch my breath. My daughter shrieks. We must come and see what she has found. At first we don't see anything. It looks like a pile of sticks and brownish leaves. She insists. "It's there." Then we see the camouflaged creature, its wrinkled head the same charcoal gray as the scattered sticks, the rusty patterns on its body like the fallen leaves. My Aunty Daphne discovers later on a Facebook reptile group that it's a mountain dragon. Sometimes it takes a child to teach us how to notice.

This trail is on the unceded lands of the Darug and Gundungurra peoples who occupied this place for tens of thousands of years. Before invasion, the Darug and Gundungurra peoples carried out regular cultural burnings as a way of caring for the land. Fires were used to encourage new growth and protect habitat. After the country was colonized by the British in 1788, European settlers destroyed major areas of natural forest and dispossessed the Aboriginal people of their lands. Aboriginal people were prohibited from doing cultural burnings. Western fire management regimes are a poor substitute – they lack intimate knowledge of the land and vegetation, and fires are often lit at the wrong time or place.

The bushfires start spreading in October. The outside air smells like woodsmoke. By November the air quality is hazardous. We drive the children the five minutes to school rather than walk. We wear face masks and buy an air filter for the house. I download an app called Air Visual, and all day I check the app for air quality index and PM particles. When the index goes above 50, I close the windows. When the index goes above 100, I cancel the kids' swim lessons. When it rises over 150, and a red notification "Unhealthy" flashes on my screen, we all stay indoors with the air filter on.

S asks me, "Is this what the future will be like? Bad and smoky?"

More than one hundred fires burn out of control across the state, engulfing the forested coastal regions, the valleys, and the Blue Mountains. On social media, people share images of neon orange and blood red skies. The news headlines read Apocalyptic, Unprecedented, Catastrophic. We watch in horror to see footage of the mountains set ablaze.

MOTHERS UNEARTHED

All summer, I have cousins, friends, and colleagues who are being evacuated from their homes. I grew up surrounded by cousins in Sydney, enough cousins to form a cricket team. But the investor-driven, wildly inflated housing market has made living in the city unaffordable for many of them. My cousin Vasant and his family moved out to the Blue Mountains. His brother Ravi and family live in Wollongong. Many people, especially migrants and the working class, have been pushed to the periphery of the city where they are at greater risk of extreme heat, bushfires, and floods. Vasant, his partner and three kids have to evacuate their house multiple times during the bushfires, for weeks at a time.

My sister and her family are visiting from LA. Six months from now, parts of their neighborhood of Monrovia will be evacuated as a result of Bobcat fires fanned by the Santa Ana winds. For most of the summer, we are indoors. My nephew K stays with us, and he and S do legos and build towers and play board games. I sit in front of a fan, the air filter turned on. It is a luxury. From my window, I can see the construction workers on a nearby site and the Indian Uber delivery guys who live next door. Not everyone can stay indoors.

New Years Eve is a sombre occasion. The state government goes ahead with their festive fireworks, but no one is in the mood. We are glued to our screens, watching the terrifying events unfolding across the country. In the beach town of Mallacoota, an out of control fire has come right up to the town and residents are ordered to leave their homes and get in the water. The world sees images of thousands of people taking refuge in the lakes and ocean under eerily crimson skies, even as temperatures dip overnight.

On New Years Day, I see on Twitter that my friend Dany who lives on a farm down south has lost several of her animals to the fires. I text her to see if she is okay and she responds:

The devastation is unfathomable. So much death. Entire eco-worlds are gone. Human communities where everyone is lost and animal communities all dead. We evacuated to Sydney last night and as I lay not sleeping and the fireworks went off I knew I was in a war. My rage is murderous but I'm also very determined not to lose this searing focus. I can't imagine how our kids are making sense of this world.

By the time all of the fires were put out in March 2020, over a billion animals were killed and three billion birds, mammals, and reptiles were displaced. While the loss of 8,000 endangered koalas had a striking impact, less cuddly species like the micro-trapdoor spider and the assassin spider may have been quietly made extinct.

In July, we go back to the Grand Canyon trail. The bushfires tore through here and the trail has been closed until now. The area is unrecognizable. All around us are the blackened trunks and charred remains of trees. The birdsong is gone. Fallen burnt logs litter the ground. It's a crisp winter day and we rub our hands together to keep warm.

I study the faces of my children. They are taking it all in. As their mama, perhaps I cannot always shelter them from climate crises. But I can show them beauty, let them know it deeply, so they may witness what is being taken from the world.

* * *

I have a recurring dream. In one version, I am driving with my children up the side of a mountain and the rain comes down heavily. The water level is rising. I drive higher to take the kids out of danger. In another version, we are home and the fire is coming closer. I grab my children and we try to escape the burning flames.

My impulse to flee with my children, to protect them, has a long lineage. My dreams carry me down the generations. My own ancestors were forced to flee their lands in Goa during the seventeenth and eighteenth centuries due to religious persecution by the Portuguese rulers, or famine, or invasion by Maratha warriors. They left their houses and fields in the middle of the night, took their babies, and sailed on old patmari boats down the coast to the Mangalore region. Even in the new country there was no peace. During the British invasion, the Goan migrants were taken into captivity by the local ruler. Again they escaped, fleeing across the Western Ghat mountains with their bundles and their children. To this day we have continued dispersing and migrating. Colonialism and extractive capitalism altered our ancestral homes and livelihoods; our history has been one of continual flight.

East Coast, Australia, April 2022

After the bushfires stopped, the rains began. At first we were grateful for the relief of water to break the long drought, the reservoirs filling and plants reviving. But the extreme and continuous rains result in dangerous flash flooding. For two years in a row we have back-to-back La Niña events, where changes in ocean currents result in increased rainfall. With global temperatures rising, these events are more intense.

Beginning in February, the unrelenting rain is punctuated by severe storms where heavy torrential rain falls quickly, leading to unpredictable flooding. Again the news headlines scream out at us. 100-year storm.

Unprecedented. Catastrophic.

I worry about our children taking public transport to school. After ten year old S is trapped on a train for one hour due to flooding on the tracks, I start driving him to school. When the flood waters are too deep to drive through, I keep the kids home.

The basement in our new rental house floods five times. The first time, we are up until midnight, removing the water in buckets, trying to salvage our possessions. Our fledgling garden does not survive. All of the peppers, basil, radishes, spinach, tomato plants, and lettuce that I planted with the children in January have washed away. We replace the air purifiers with dehumidifiers as creeping mold and mildew infests our home. We learn to live with the huntsman spiders who come seeking refuge. We too are privileged to hunker down indoors. We consider ourselves lucky to even have a home.

The flooding devastation spreads all along the East Coast through the states of New South Wales and Queensland. Twenty-two people are killed, tens of thousands lose their homes, and whole towns are submerged.

In early March, my Uncle Ritchie, eighty years old and blind, along with my Aunty Nanda and their daughter Priya, also with disability, are trapped in their home up north in Brisbane when the waters begin rising. The flood waters submerge the ground floor of their house and come almost up to the second story. They pack a go bag, and clear the furniture near the bedroom window in case they need to escape onto the roof over the carport. The emergency services are overwhelmed with calls from people needing to be rescued. By 9pm the waters begin to recede and the next day they are able to leave by the front door and evacuate.

In the light of morning, the extent of the damage is apparent. Behind the house was a sprawling garden where Aunty Nanda grew okra, gourd, karela, lokhi, and spinach from her native Fiji. She had over a hundred chilli plants, dragonfruit, a pumpkin patch, asparagus, melons, blueberries, potatoes and beans as well as avocado, mango, lime, and lemon trees. The garden was a space where neighbors and local communities of Filipinos, Indians, Fijians and others came to get produce they couldn't find elsewhere. It was a place of exchange, a lifeline for many at a time of increasing cost of living, and a way for Aunty Nanda to keep active in her retirement. It took years to plant and nurture some of these crops. The garden is flooded by salt water. Aunty Nanda watches the plants die and shrivel in a few hours.

My relatives, and many others are asking, will this happen again? Should we move? Where to move when surrounding areas are flooded too? My cousin Priya says to me, "Where can you go where you won't be affected?" The question is poignant. I recall visits from Uncle Ritchie as a child, how he spoke with such longing for our hometown of Mangalore, a place he never wanted to leave. I think about Aunty Nanda, a descendant of indentured laborers brought from India to Fiji. How long can you keep moving till there is nowhere left to move?

* * *

During the coronavirus pandemic, mass climate rallies switch to online Zoom rallies and digital actions. At an online protest of the Adani mining corporation's occupation of Wangan and Jagalingou lands, I see the schoolgirls who have gathered in an empty gym. I see the elderly matrons who have brought their neighbors to a community center to join in the protest. I see the geoscientist logging in from Godda, India, where Adani plans to transport the coal to a power station built on the lands of the Santhal people. I see Wangan and Jagalingou elder Adrian Burragubba speak of what his country is like: the life-giving Doongmabulla Springs teeming with waxy cabbage palms, brolgas, and emus.

I see the other mamas. I recognize their distraction as they issue muted orders to someone offscreen, a child's head occasionally popping into the frame. I know the look of determination, the fury we nurture as our weapon and our power.

Together we flood the inboxes of Adani investors to tell them they do not have the informed consent of the Wangan and Jagalingou people to go ahead with their coal mine. We write to the Queensland environment minister demanding that he protect the sacred Doongmabulla Springs. We send dozens of email invites to the State Bank of India, clogging up their calendars. We make donations and we post on social media and we write poetry and we join our bodies to the Wangan and Jagalingou camp on the grounds of the mining site.

Alongside the squares of faces and groups on Zoom, I see the now familiar chat box fill with messages of solidarity. Refuge might look like this. Apart but connected on this planet.

Concerning the Sea Stars
Deesha Philyaw

MONDAY 3:27 PM

Incoming message from Mom: You sure you don't want a party for your birthday? Thirteen is a big one. . .

Cleo: I'm sure

Mom: Okay. . .

Mom: Let me know if you change your mind.

Mom: Grandma is going to bring potato salad and macaroni and cheese. Your favorites.

Cleo: ok

Mom: And I'm going to get some ribs and chicken from that place you like on Ardmore.

Cleo: ok

Mom: Do you want a white lily cake from Food Glorious Food, or do you want Grandma to bake you a chocolate cake? She offered.

MONDAY 4:13 PM

Meredith: Hello?

Meredith: Cleo, what's the matter?

MONDAY 4:20 PM

Cleo: Nothing. I fell asleep.
Meredith: What kind of cake do you want?
Cleo: Doesn't matter.
Meredith: But it's your birthday.

MONDAY 5:01 PM

Meredith: Cleo?

~

TUESDAY 3:18 PM

Keith: What time is Cleo's birthday dinner again?
Meredith: 6:00
Keith: Saturday?
Meredith: No, Friday. You agreed to let her stay for dinner and join us, rather than picking her up at the usual time. Saturday is her birthday.
Keith: I know Saturday's her birthday. I was there.
Meredith: <thumbs up emoji>
Keith: Jamilah is coming to dinner with me.
Meredith: <thumbs down emoji>
Meredith: It's a ***family*** birthday dinner. And I already told you, it's not good for Cleo to be caught up in the revolving door of our dating lives.

MOTHERS UNEARTHED

Keith: You seeing somebody, Meredith?

Meredith: You're missing the point.

Keith: Ah so you're not dating anyone LOL

Meredith: WTF? Are you 12???? Divorce is a trauma for our child. We've been separated for less than three months. Cleo needs time to heal.

Keith: Let me guess: You read that in one of those co-parenting books.

Meredith: Yes, I did. But you don't have to believe me. Just talk to Cleo's therapist. I gave you her number.

Keith: I know my kid. I don't need a therapist, or a book, or you, telling me that I'm a bad father.

Meredith: No one is saying you're a bad father. I'm just saying again that Cleo doesn't need to be around anyone you're dating. Or anyone I'm dating. It's too soon.

Keith: She's already met Jamilah.

Meredith: And she shouldn't have.

Keith: Here we go. . .

Meredith: Yes, here we fucking go. Cleo doesn't need to know anything about your dating life at this point. Like I told you before: she doesn't get another childhood. This is it. Five more years. Would it have killed you to wait until she's not so tender?

Keith: Like you waited to pull the plug on our family?

Meredith: I pulled the plug on our *marriage*. Big difference.

Keith: I think you're the one who's tender. And bitter and mad. Well, be mad at yourself. I want Jamilah to know and Cleo to know AND YOU TO KNOW that I've moved on.

Meredith: FOR THE FIFTYLEVENTH TIME I don't give a flying fuck that you're dating someone! Just keep Cleo out of it. Yes, as you reminded me, you don't need my permission. Rushing this is going to backfire on you. If you pump the brakes now, you'll be giving a relationship between Cleo and Jamilah a fighting chance, in the long run.

Keith: LOL. Like you care about their relationship having a fighting chance.

Meredith: I care about what's best for Cleo. And you introducing her to someone soon after you left isn't in her best interest.

Keith: You say that like I just up and moved out one day! You wanted this, not me!

Meredith: I didn't want it to be like this. Cleo is really struggling. She barely comes out of her room, doesn't want to eat, doesn't want to spend time with her friends anymore. I have to beg her to do her homework. Textbook signs of depression.

Keith: YOU wanted this, and now you're surprised that our child of divorce is showing signs of being a child of divorce.

Meredith: But it doesn't have to be as bad as you've made it by introducing your girlfriend so soon.

Keith: You're the one with the problem: bitterness, regret, loneliness. Cleo is fine! She likes Jamilah. They have fun. And at my house, Cleo eats, she does her homework, and she invites friends over.

Meredith: PLEASE! Do you even know her friends' pronouns?

Keith: Pronouns???

Meredith: Cleo breezed through her honors classes last trimester, but now her grades have dropped. She's in danger of failing. Which you would know if you ever checked the parent portal.

Keith: Go to hell.

Meredith: Go to therapy.

Subject: Cleo's birthday   Sun, Feb. 13, 10:31 PM
From: Meredith Sharpe <msharpewilson@gmail.com>
To: Keith Wilson <wilsonkl767@gmail.com>

Keith:

Do you remember Cleo's first birthday party? She kept tugging off her party shoes and ended up running around barefoot the whole time? The theme was fairies, and I dressed us both like Tinkerbell. Remember I got you that male fairy costume, but your outdated notions about masculinity wouldn't allow you to wear it? Not even to make special memories for your child?

Remember Cleo's third birthday party and how I transformed the first floor into the Hundred Acre Wood for a classic Winnie the Pooh-themed party? The living room, with couch cushions, bedroom pillows, and throw pillows piled high, was the area with *Big Stones and Rocks*, a perfect place for jumps and soft landings? Remember how Cleo called to us as she bounced, *"MommyDaddy*, look at me, *MommyDaddy!"*

because we were, for her, a single unit of love? And remember how your mother pretended she couldn't remember my "white girl" name? We had been married for five years at that point. And remember how she complained loudly in front of our guests? "Back in the day," she said, "we gave them kids hot dogs and Lays potato chips, and got a cake from the grocery store and one of them cartons of ice cream with the chocolate, vanilla, and strawberry in it." [It's called Neapolitan.] "Now *that* was a birthday party," your mother said. "This" — and she gestured then at our build-your-own-taco bar and the miniature "hunny" pots filled with dulce de leche ice cream lining the dining room table — "This is just putting on airs, Marigold."

God rest your mother's soul, but she was a witch.

And I'm sure you remember Cleo's fifth birthday. The cracks were just starting to show in our marriage, and you got this wild hair to organize Cleo's party. Not because you gave a shit about the parties or had any organizational skills whatsoever. No, you insisted on planning the party and refused any help from me, all because I innocently mentioned that I was tired of doing all the mental and emotional labor for our family, including event planning. Your exact words were: "You're tired because you wear yourself out putting on airs, Marigold." And you cracked yourself up laughing.

But that wasn't funny. At all. You (and your mother, rest her rotten soul) have always mistaken care, thoughtfulness, foresight, and attention to detail for "putting on airs." What you consider extra, I consider essential. In layman's terms, you're a cheap bastard and you're careless with people's hearts, Keith. And careless in general. Which is why the guests you invited to Cleo's party all arrived at the house the weekend *before* Cleo's birthday instead of the weekend of her birthday.

Remember how you left me to set out cans of barely cold La Croix and bowls of microwave popcorn, while you ran out to the store to get hot dogs, Lays, a cake (Happy Birthday, Theo???), and Neapolitan ice cream?

Then there was Cleo's 10 ½ birthday which we celebrated that August because she wanted to have a pool party. I doubt you and I spoke more than 10 words to each other the entire day. But Cleo was happy. She no longer called us *MommyDaddy*. She'd outgrown that. And, perhaps, she knew even then that we were no longer a unit.

But I like to think that she knew right up to the end that we remained united in our love for her, that we both endeavored to do what was best for her, albeit separately. Last year, at her birthday sleepover, we made a joint appearance when it was time to sing Happy Birthday and eat cake. And then we returned to our respective corners. I don't know if Cleo will remember that.

But we both know what Cleo is going to remember about her 13th birthday. She's going to remember how you treated her and her besties to a spa day complete with a three-tiered princess cake and pizza for lunch, and a limo ride. She's going to remember how after you and Jamilah dropped off her last friend, you popped a bottle of champagne in the back of that limo and announced your engagement. *On her birthday.*

On. Her. Birthday.

While we're still legally married.

Have you completely lost your mind?

I'm so angry right now, I'm shaking. Are you trying to hurt your daughter? Because that's what's happened.

And save the bullshit about how CLEO IS FINE. Cleo is absolutely NOT fine. Of course she's not going to tell you how she feels. She knows you expect her to be happy for you. She doesn't want to risk upsetting you. Besides, when would she even have a chance to talk to you about anything when, apparently, Jamilah never leaves your side and Cleo hasn't been alone with you in weeks?

You have five years to make this right instead of making it worse. Please, for Cleo's sake, rethink this. She needs you to do right by her. She's already struggling. I know you don't believe me. Call the school guidance counselor. Make an appointment for family counseling. If you don't want me there, fine. Just go with Cleo. Please, Keith. Do what's best for Cleo.

~M

Subject: Re: Cleo's birthday   Mon, Feb. 14, 12:17 PM
From: Keith Wilson <wilsonkl767@gmail.com>
To: Meredith Sharpe <msharpewilson@gmail.com>

Dear Meredith:

Keith is not interested in traveling down memory lane with you. (This is Jamilah.)

We should meet. I tried to say "hi" the last time you came to pick up Cleo but you drove off before I could make it down the driveway. What are you afraid of, Meredith? The future? I'm Cleo's future, and, by extension, yours too. And the future is bright, so you should embrace it/me.

Speaking of me, I'm the newest cast member on the hit reality TV show *Keeping Up with the Real Second Wives Who Bake*. We haven't taped any episodes yet because the producers won't film Cleo without both parents' permission. All the paperwork is attached, along with an NDA for both you and Cleo. Please sign at your earliest convenience, no later than Friday. Shooting begins the following Monday. We can't imagine doing this without Cleo; her age demographic does extremely well with test audiences. You know, teen angst and rebellion, or whatever. And apparently dogs test better than cats, but the producers said that my kitty Badu stays in the picture! (Get it? I love old Hollywood!)

Anyway… I don't mean to be dismissive of your concerns. I too am a child of divorce. My parents divorced twenty years ago and hated each other the way they were supposed to. And look at me! I turned out just fine. Friendliness between you and Keith would be confusing for Cleo. Besides, conflict between the two of you will guarantee that we'll be featured in every episode!

By the way, I'm encouraging Keith to file for 50-50 custody. This every-other-weekend arrangement isn't going to yield enough footage.

I know what you're thinking, and I'm sure I can get the producers to script in a man for you. But, and I say this gently, you will first need to do something about your weight. My sister, who is your age, refers to her belly fat as her COVID-19 baby. But that was three pandemics ago, and none of this is a laughing matter. Thankfully, I have managed to keep a flat tummy, all praises to Pilates, waist trainers, and intermittent fasting. Follow my fitness journey on Instagram; I know you stalk me there anyway.

Did Keith tell you how we met? I was just about to delete the Afrindr app (it's Tinder for people of the African Diaspora). Because every guy I matched with couldn't spell my name or couldn't afford my bills (or both!). And then there was Keith. His profile was so sweet! "Anyone looking for a good man? A workout buddy? Or maybe nice guys really do finish last…" Meredith, you set that man out on the curb like a gently used piece of Arhaus furniture. Well, you know what they say: One woman's trash is another woman's new Mercedes G-Wagon. (Keith got it for me for our two-month anniversary!)

But everything happens for a reason. Keith and I were meant to be. Even our names are perfect for the spin-off reality show I'm manifesting for us: *Jamilah and Keith: something-something- something.* It's giving very 90s Black rom-com, no? *Meredith and Keith* . . . sounds like a biracial couple who wear garden clogs and own an Old English sheepdog. Plus, you're both engineers; too matchy-matchy.

I heard you and Cleo have a little girls' getaway planned for the long weekend. Private beach! Nice. That would be a perfect place for a let's-try-to-bond-but-it-all-falls-apart scene for the three of us. I'll send a note to the producers.

Have a safe trip and be sure to send me the signed paperwork before you hit the road!

Warmly,
Jamilah

P.S. How do I go about resetting Keith's password to the parent portal? He can't find the email from the school.

P.P.S. Happy Valentine's Day!

~

MONDAY 11:01 PM

Meredith: It's highly inappropriate for your girlfriend to contact me. I won't be responding to that email.
Keith: What email?

~

Subject: Re: Cleo's birthday   Tue, Feb. 15, 12:48 AM
From: Keith Wilson <wilsonkl767@gmail.com>
To: Meredith Sharpe <msharpewilson@gmail.com>

Dear Meredith:

Snitches get stitches! LOL j/k

Just a gentle reminder from your friendly neighborhood IG model-turned-reality TV star (soon to be!). Can you sign the papers already? :)

Warmly,
Jamilah

~

TUESDAY 12:54 AM

Meredith: Please retrieve your balls from your girlfriend's purse and tell her to leave me alone. If she persists in harassing me, perhaps a family court judge can assist you in getting her to stop. It's certainly not in Cleo's best interest to be around someone so unhinged. I've blocked your email address. If you need to reach me for any matter concerning Cleo, text me.

Keith: So now you're mad I bought her a Coach purse

Meredith: Wait what?

~

Subject: Guess who!   Wed, Feb. 16, 6:11 AM
From: Future Mrs. Wilson <bookings@jamilahluxurious.com>
To: Meredith Sharpe <msharpewilson@gmail.com>

Meredith:

It's in Cleo's best interest that we remain cordial. So I'm asking nicely… this time. Please send the signed paperwork and the information re: the parent portal.

TIA,
Jamilah

~

WEDNESDAY 6:19 AM

Meredith: Your lawyer will be hearing from mine. Tell your dingbat girlfriend that I said thanks for sending me all that ammo.
Keith: Is that a threat?
Meredith: No, it's a promise.

~

SATURDAY 7:46 AM

Meredith: I went out for a walk on the beach. Didn't want you to be alarmed if you woke up while I was out. There are starfish everywhere out here. Overnight hundreds of them washed ashore. You should come see.

SATURDAY 8:01 AM

Cleo: Sea stars
Meredith: ?
Cleo: Sea stars is their proper name, not starfish
Meredith: Oh! You learn something new everyday. I heard this story once about a man who was walking along the beach after a bad storm. A bunch of sea creatures washed up the shore, and the man could tell they were either dead or

dying. He noticed a little boy throwing some of the starfish back into the ocean…

Meredith: *SEA STARS back into the ocean. The man asked the boy why he was wasting his time. There were thousands of stranded sea stars on the shore; he couldn't possibly save them all. "So what you're doing doesn't matter, in the grand scheme of things," the man told the boy.

Meredith: The boy picked up a struggling sea star, tossed it into the ocean and said, "It mattered to that one."

Meredith: Are you dressed? Come down and help me? There aren't thousands here, but definitely hundreds.

Meredith: <sends photo of the stranded sea stars>

Cleo: Don't touch them!!!!!!

Meredith: Why not???

Cleo: First of all, their arms are fragile. They can regenerate, but handling and throwing them can easily hurt or damage them. Plus, we have billions of bacteria on our hands that can kill them.

Meredith: Wow.

Meredith: Sometimes it's easy to hurt even when you're trying to help.

Cleo: Like you telling me I can't see dad anymore until you go to court?

Meredith: Yeah. Like that. I'm so sorry, Cleo. Your dad isn't using the best judgment right now, and I have to protect you. And you and me… we have to communicate. We have to be honest

with each other about what's going on. Even
when it's hard.

Cleo: Yeah right <eye roll emoji>

Meredith: ???

Cleo: You told me that you and Dad made the
decision together. You said, "Sometimes parents
have grown-up problems that they work hard to
fix. For years. But no matter how hard they try,
the problems remain. And we've decided to get
a divorce." No, Mom. YOU wanted a divorce. You
lied.

Meredith: Where is all of this coming from,
Cleo?

Cleo: Jamilah told me the truth.

Subject: Re: Guess who! Sat, Feb. 19, 8:49 AM

From: Meredith Sharpe <msharpewilson@gmail.com>
To: Future Mrs. Wilson <bookings@jamilahluxurious.com>

Let me tell you one goddamn thing: If you contact my daughter again,
the first episode of that reality show will feature your funeral.

You asked what I'm afraid of. Only two things: 1) That I will catch a case
behind this bullshit with you and Keith and won't be around to see my
child grow up. 2) And yes, the future. I'm terrified that you and Keith
are ruining Cleo's life. That she feels abandoned by him and usurped by
you. That she will go looking for love in all the wrong places. That she
will feel worthless. That, as a result, she will become a junkie prostitute.
All because you and her father are too childish and self-absorbed to
consider what's best for her.

Fuck all the way off (and that includes you too, Keith),
Meredith

P. S. It will be a cold day in hell before I help you access the parent portal.

~

SATURDAY 8:22 PM

Meredith: Please come down and eat something, honey.
Cleo: I told you I'm not hungry.
Meredith: Okay. The seafood linguini is in the fridge, if you change your mind. Love you.

SATURDAY 10:35 PM

Cleo: Do you even know why so many sea stars are out there?
Meredith: No...
Cleo: Climate change. Warmer water, changing current patterns, more hurricanes... all of that pushes them ashore. It's not something that happened overnight. Last trimester, I did a report on this for my environmental science class. You were traveling a lot that month. Dad helped me with it.
Meredith: Oh, I didn't realize that he helped you. I'd love to read your report, if you

wouldn't mind sharing it.

Cleo: Ok. I'll email you the link.

~

MONDAY 7:11 PM

Meredith: I never wanted some random judge making decisions for our family. But here we are.

Meredith: I don't want to fight with you. But if that's what it takes to help Cleo heal, I will.

Meredith: In the meantime, it's not right for me to keep her from you. I warned you that these next five years are critical, that Cleo is counting on us to protect her and help her thrive, that if we don't act in her best interest, she will continue to suffer. So now I'm going to heed my own warnings.

Meredith: I'm still so angry with you that I could spit.

Keith: Take a number. Jamilah's mad at me too.

Meredith: Oh?

Keith: Yeah. Without you and Cleo, the producers weren't interested in having her on the reality show.

Meredith: Oh…

Meredith: I could be really, really petty right now, but I won't.

Keith: Thank you.

Unconscious

Nimmi Gowrinathan

"I gift you two worlds, this dance, this arrival to yourself regardless of the thousand inevitable little leavings you are forced to live through.

Remember, home is the ocean within, endless is the swimming.

Home is the ocean...
endless—

He bids me to swim, i sink."

- Enbah Nilah

His fishhooks, snagged in a couch cushion or the lining of a hoodie, have littered our homes for years. My son catches my ire more often than large-mouthed bass.

One afternoon, well after I instituted the (failed) Ban on Fishing Paraphernalia in the New House, his indoor casting practice snags the edge of a rug brought as a gift from Iran. The textured fabric was just settling into a comfortable flatness after a cramped return journey filling the void of Tums bottles and other mundane contraband smuggled in outbound luggage from America. The rug conforms to my home's unintentional design: elevating reminders of suffering on the outside above any interior aesthetic vision. I give my son a look but say nothing as he works quickly to untangle the hook. Activists and mothers learn to pick their battles.

The pole, meant for fly fishing, is my son's latest acquisition, joining the gaggle of other fishing devices forced to tolerate a groping curiosity that mangles their parts. Certain the new purchase will keep him occupied, buying me a few moments of mid-day silence, I sit across the room, reading an article on climate justice.

Happily freed from focused supervision, he swings the elongated stick around again. When the weather and his mother limit his access to the water, he fishes at home. Watching the rod extend from wall to wall, his imagination stretches to fill with waders and new lures. He barely notices the tip knock the art carefully hung above the Iranian rug.

In the lounge chair (that in practice is a jumpseat for surveilling the children in the living room), I am taken by how Anna Badhken writes of the Spanish acquisition of Mexican land in her essay for Adi Magazine. "The landscape of their imagining was devoid of human life, and their maps called the land El Despoblado: The Unpeopled." Her words draw ecocide and genocide closer together—closing a gap I've unconsciously maintained. My unapologetic pre-occupation has always been the disposal of human life in pursuit of dominance—in America and Sri Lanka.

I hear my son's stick hit glass. He hears me yell. The over-enunciated consonants in his name startle him. He sighs, puts down his stick, and picks up his own reading. The book is his own stuffed tiger—his tattered copy of *The Essential Calvin and Hobbes* dragged alongside him as the loyal ally of the perpetually misunderstood.

I get up and carefully reposition the piece on the wall. The art itself has escaped his child's-eye-view of his world. Like the strings of a worn sari, a net made of straggles of coconut fibers is captured in still frame. Delicately painted in the middle of the repurposed net, turned upright, is a very stern-looking fish.

* * *

European-oriented psychoanalysis believed the mind to be divided into three parts: conscious, subconscious, and unconscious. Freud likened the parsing to an iceberg, with the tip (only ten percent) visible and readily available to us as consciousness. The bulk of the mind, then, is completely submerged in the deep recesses of unconsciousness, with pre-conscious thoughts floating just below the sea line.

* * *

"The sea is broken, fishermen say. The sea is empty. The genii have taken the fish elsewhere." - Anna Badhken, author and journalist

I have indulged his fishing obsession since he was five. Sensing he had prematurely located his own natural peace, I took him to scout the lakes, streams, and oceans on three continents. He covered as many American states as he could cajole a license-bearing adult into accompanying him. Some children ask questions; mine makes statements. He took to lecturing from a young age. As the offspring of two academics, he may have been committing an act of mirroring, rebellion, or both. He was five when his father and I separated, and he needed things to have a proper place. In the tiny apartment where we landed after the breakup, he noticed cardboard mixed in with regular trash, and scolded me.

I was taken aback. Not by the reprimand itself (*You're not thinking about the planet you're leaving us!*), but by this child's emerging consciousness. The jolt tapped into my endless reservoirs of guilt, unsettling a question that flitted in and out of my mind when confronted with some upcycled detergent-box-turned-clutch that was the face of a consumer-driven environmentalist movement in America.

Why wasn't I, as an activist, more invested in the environment? Reparations for those sunken in mass graves shouldn't preclude healthy air for the living?

Anna Badhken asks, "What does unpeopling a place permit?" and answers, "It permits exploitation and erasure of environments and the human communities these environments contain and sustain."

* * *

The fish on the wall is a gray mullet, one of the native species disappearing from the Batticaloa lagoon in Eastern Sri Lanka. The artist highlighted the loss in order to draw out the plight of his people—taken in large numbers by the military—without being vanished himself. Undocumented violence made visible by the disappeared.

My earliest work, nearly two decades ago now, focused on Tamil girls on the cusp of adulthood who fought for their lives, and their land, as women. When I met them, they had moved off the battlefield into a children's home lining the Batticaloa lagoon famous in local lore for fish that sing. The children mapped their own journey, pushed from inland homes into a resistance movement, with cartographic precision:

moments of war in interior villages became landmarks on the terrain of nascent memories. A father killed by the Sri Lankan army, a mother cast off as "unwell," an uncle prone to abusive bouts of PTSD.

When he was eight, old enough to accompany me to sift through the wreckage of defeat, my son and I had driven past miles of land emptied by war, its traditional inhabitants forcefully moved to inhospitable territory. When we reached the sunlit zones just north of the Batticaloa lagoon, my son convinced his grandfather (to my relief) to join him on a hotel-arranged excursion into the same edges of the Indian Ocean his ancestors on both bordering land masses had fished. He returned dejected, as he always was when his oceanic comrades refused to reveal themselves. There were no fish left to catch.

A genii, in Islamic mythology, is a supernatural creature, beyond scientific understanding. In Kashmir, a mother leaves all her doors ajar in anticipation of her son's return. The state, activist Ather Zia notes, "makes a disappearance appear as an aberration of dubious origin, rather than a deliberate punishment."

At an age where child-like curiosity was beginning to fade, my son seemed to accept the cries of mothers sitting in a lagoon-adjacent temple in Sri Lanka whose children have been disappeared by the military as natural. A part of this thing called war. But he cannot understand why the army would destroy the natural habitat of the fish.

* * *

Some scientists believe imagination exists at a level below conscious awareness. Others feel it is burrowed much deeper in the unconscious, emerging from thoughts and feelings unavailable to introspection. "To imagine is to represent without aiming at things as they actually, presently, and subjectively are.[1]

* * *

After his summer in Sri Lanka, in fourth grade, my son organized his own action—starting a petition to end the use of plastic utensils at his Bronx elementary school. He realized, he tells me, that the climate crisis meant the fish might disappear completely by the time he had children. "How will my grandchildren fish?" he asks. A condemnation masquerading as a question.

I begin to be performatively thoughtful in the everyday. Carefully folding cardboard and sorting plastics in a series of household micromovements that placate his demands for individual action yet seem tenuously tied to my commitment to collective resistance. "Too many people are blissfully ignorant," he opines with a smugness lined with a hint of the joy so easily available to him. Without the weight of self-consciousnesses, every childhood thought bubbles to the surface. He is his own omniscient narrator.

* * *

Wherever I settle to work, I place a picture of a child in an oversized red shirt half-smiling as I bounce a yellow ball to him. My own silhouette is blurred, but the child's gaze is a lucid mix of fear and joy. My son had always been curious about this print that had followed us from my desk in our shared bedroom to our new house. Who was this child, he asks, who I was so attached to? This child who wasn't my son?

---

1 Kind, A. "Can imagination be unconscious?" *Synthese* 199, 13121–13141 (2021). https://doi.org/10.1007/s11229-021-03369-0

MOTHERS UNEARTHED

I had told him about a tsunami that ejected the Batticaloa lagoon onto land, obliterating a habited coastline. He was intrigued, as he always was, with what he called "weather events." When a flash hurricane caused water to drip into our living room, he ran between windowsills with a bucket. He carefully tracked the inches predicted and produced by a snowstorm and always called from his father's house down the street to inform me that hail was falling in a slanted attack on old windows. Without a concerted effort on his part, these moments felt as if nature was speaking, just to him.

I would try to tell him about the little boy in the red t-shirt, about the people in refugee camps moved inland, but his eyes widened when I told him about the sea. "It really turned black? Thirty feet high?" Questions to confirm what he already knew. His face crashed with a sudden realization: "Think of all the fish that died."

The art from the lagoon hangs in our home just as the artist insisted that it should. The image of the fish is placed vertically, like the stiff Tamil portrait of a loved one gone too soon—not horizontally as the fish might freely exist.

* * *

The unconscious mind exists outside conscious awareness. It holds biological instincts for survival, aggression, protection. It is often described as a reservoir of unpleasant feelings tied to pain, anxiety, and conflict.

* * *

When chaos, and violence, erupts, women are attached to their children.

Women and children are elevated above the general fray of suffering to raise funds, evoke empathy, and trigger a collective responsibility to protect. In the years after the Boxing Day Tsunami, before my son was born, I watched as humanitarians flooded the children's home after the lagoon settled back into place. Young women were offered crayons, older women sewing machines—both, in their own way, "infantilized." To infantilize women is to treat them as a being with no emotional awareness or insight: to treat them as one would a child. Children, by universal consensus (should?) have no politics.

As the aid workers invaded, the military recharged. In the chaos of a natural disaster, lines of political control for territories once firmly under the grip of the resistance began to blur. The artist notes the introduction of a new kind of net, with finer meshes than traditional hand-woven coconut fiber. Powered by military-grade strength, smaller local species were rounded up en masse.

When the water temperature rose in the lagoon, the fish moved to the bottom in search of oxygen. As the war closed in, the people dug bunkers deep in the sand. White phosphorus burned human flesh and built up inside the bodies of marine animals. As the military occupied Tamil homelands, it introduced a dominant species in the lagoon—one that fed off of indigenous fish.

Traditional inhabitants, both disappeared in plain sight while the children watched.

* * *

Just below sea level, the preconscious is immediately available and accessible to inform a conscious awareness. Thoughts and feelings float freely, unrepressed,

MOTHERS UNEARTHED

but not fully realized.

* * *

When he was six, not much older than the boy with the red shirt in the refugee camp, after our first few failed fishing excursions, I bought my son a net. My theory was that if his little hands couldn't yet master the precision of string and bait, the wide expanse of the net (often dunked along with the right side of his body) might yield a few tiny friends in local beaches and shallow tide pools.

Years later, as he became marginally more skilled in his passion, he sought out live bait to dangle below the glittery lures he'd spent his allowance on. On the way to brunch one day in city-adjacent rural America, he convinced me to stop at a tackle shop to procure a bucket of minnows that I insisted remain in the car.

As the human adults sipped their way through a slow meal, he grew anxious. He fidgeted and asked if he could return to the car. When he returned his eyes were welling with tears willed not to fall out of deference to his near-tween status. Both frustrated and concerned, I asked what was happening. He sighed and explained.

"The oxygen inside the car is limited, mom. The top layers of the water in the bucket are getting warm, and the fish are already moving to the bottom to find air. One is already dead. Can I please sit with them on the sidewalk?"

That afternoon, before he set off with the remaining minnows, my son, now a fisherman, insisted I not say "good luck," but, rather, "tight lines,"—a phrase that evokes for me the thick blue string tripping me in the house, not the fleeting moments a fish was drawn to this child's carefully chosen lure.

* * *

The conscious mind holds perceptions, sensations, rational thoughts and feelings that occupy a hyper-present awareness.

* * *

My son scours National Geographic media and YouTube, alternating between fishing hacks and understanding why the floor of the sea is rumbling and its surface rising. His privilege allows him to build awareness behind a screen that others in his generational cohort experience as a relentless lived reality.

The young women who startle easily and battle nightmares in Sri Lanka tell me, "I keep wondering when the next attack will be," their fears distributed equally between water and land. In Palestine, a ten-year-old child pleads with the world to grapple with the destruction she is forced to exist inside. "This isn't fair. It just isn't fair," she repeats, a clear thought against a background of chaos. In Colombia, an unarmed nine-year old girl playing is presumed to be a "machine of war." With her friends watching, she was killed in one of several government attacks during a ceasefire. For these children, toxic moments deplete protective layers, leaving an indelible imprint of trauma.

For all children, pressure builds as submerged anxieties demand a release: a deep angst begins to shake within. Unformed thoughts on equality and justice displace a pristine vision of the horizon. Lines are blurred as consciousness expands, visible as both a developmental milestone and political threat.

MOTHERS UNEARTHED

Every disaster is created by adults. In most countries, in this country, the narrative shelter of childhood is the only shield offered to them. As with other displaced selves, they barter their claim to a complete humanity for any temporary refuge. The interlocked existence of a people and their place swirls inside the children closest to the earth's discontents. These children are a different type of woke—forced into a constant state of alert.

For me, questions circle in an endless loop of critical thought. Is the possibility of an evolving consciousness, if not a fully formed identity, an unfair imposition on growing internal lives… or the breathing space necessary to process their external existence? My son's every day was weighted so differently than the children I encountered—could his consciousness be lifted to correct the imbalance? Or should every mother wish for their children to live through their formative years in blissful ignorance?

* * *

Psychoanalysis drawn from thinking from lands bordering the Indian Ocean believed the unconscious to be populated by the collective, rather than limited to the individual. A collective unconscious formed through a shared set of experiences that maintained the connection between human beings and their ancestors. When it is accessed, the unconscious reveals a deep reservoir of pain.

* * *

Wartime correspondent and author Anna Badhken quoted the poetry of Pattiann Rogers to collapse the false divide between humans and nature: "Nature is what is, everything that is, everything that has been, and everything that is possible, including human actions, inventions, creations, and imaginations." For a moment in the middle of the war, the disappeared re-appeared in the lagoon. Like fish, dead bodies float to the surface. Undocumented violence made visible by the disappeared.

My son and I are both thinking about extinction: he, the fish, and I, the elimination of a people. Both evolving and oriented towards suffering, we meet in nature. The moments that his underwater friends are lured to him are a flurry of flopping fins and little hands working quickly to release them. He has never kept a fish that he caught.

Just North of Sri Lanka the glacial ice of a third pole is melting. His imagination expands as my consciousness grows. In Sri Lanka a regime committed to genocide is left without diesel to power fishing boats. Forced to sink, the fish no longer sing and only a few gray mullets remain.

Dead Deer

January Gill O'Neil

I found her on her side
    in the mucky pond behind the house,

bedded in rigor, head submerged
    but flanks exposed, covered in flies.

White tail. Little peninsula.
    Nights ago, I startled you with my headlights

as you leapt into the tall grasses,
    and each day since I waited for your return.

You made my heart skip.
    Maybe you dipped to drink

along the low bank, settled in the cool water
    to relieve some pain, some wound unseen.

What loneliness drove you
    under the low-hanging trees

and knotted roots along the bank?

Who will miss you?

When the men hauled you
    onto shore, the dragonflies swooped

and swirled the sickening heat,
    in the space your body had been.

The noonday sun is brutal;
    the pond reflects everything.

Making Our Own Weather

Claire Boyles

Pyrocumulus clouds rise above fires that burn with special intensity. The clouds are multi-colored—shades of brown and gray and white, gilded with silver—as beautiful as they are terrifying. Animate, active, full of turbulence and ice and electricity, they are powerful enough to make their own weather, and they have choices. Some generate enough rain and hail to put the fire beneath them out completely. Others create lightning that ignites more blazes, winds that blow flame into inferno— spinning vortexes called fire whirls, or firenadoes, or fire devils. They can send particulates all the way up into the lower stratosphere, or they can downdraft them powerfully back toward earth, sending embers in all directions. NASA calls them the "fire-breathing dragon of clouds."

In August of 2020, a pyrocumulus cloud appeared in the sky just as I finished pitching a tent in a state park two hours from my Colorado home. I had left a day early for our last family camping trip before my oldest left for college, a way to create my own wilderness writing residency, so I was alone at the site. The fire was far enough away that I knew I was safe, but close enough that I didn't know for how long. The rangers told me I did not have to evacuate, not yet, but the direct road home, the one I had just traveled, was already closed, clogged with evacuees and emergency vehicles. I packed up and drove toward Wyoming, taking the long way home. That fire, the Cameron Peak Fire, would become the largest in Colorado history, would burn even as it was buried under fourteen inches of snow in early September. It was not fully contained until December 2 of that year.

Already, that first day, the fire was burning into and around the Rawah Wilderness, where we'd taken our kids on their first overnight backpacking trip in 2014. They were nine and eleven. After only three miles of hiking, we found the Laramie River raging fast and deep, too swollen with snowmelt runoff to safely take the kids across. We made camp close to a game trail on which a steady stream of moose ambled down to drink from a river eddy. We chose the tent site carefully, considering which of the beetle-kill ponderosa pines, death-gray but still standing, might blow down on top of us in a windstorm. The backcountry campsite was well-used, with a fire ring made from gathered rocks in a small clearing. To pass the time, we tested shredded bark and seed pods and twigs to see which most easily caught a spark from a flint.

We took our kids into the wilderness as often as we could while they were growing up—hiking over high mountain passes, pitching tents above tree lines while coyotes yipped in the distance, cooking lean dinners on tiny stoves while constellations burned bright above us. We wanted to map wilderness onto their hearts: the effortless glide of a beaver in the pool behind its lodge, the butterscotch scent of ponderosa pines, the bitter, roaring wind that blows across the tundra and into your ears, swirling through and softening a jumpy modern mind. We taught them to stay on the trail, to leave no trace. In the face of climate catastrophe, we wanted them to love the world enough to work to save it, but we also wanted them to feel, as much as possible, the joy of being alive within it. They believed us when we told them that an official wilderness designation meant the land would be there for them far into the future, that it might be altered by climate change, but it would be intact, more or less untouched. In our defense, until these past years of mega-fires, we believed it too.

We made the entire twelve-mile trip through the Rawah two years later, post-holing through remnant snowfields that hid the trail on north facing slopes, playing cards in the tent when the evening's mosquitoes became intolerable. On that trip, we did not use the flints, did not start a fire at all, did not want to spark anything we might not be able to control. Our outdoor ethics had shifted. Fire in the backcountry had become irresponsible, and we were only ever playing at survival, after all. Those Rawah trips are some of my happiest mothering memories, and as I drove away from that fire cloud in 2020, I pictured exactly the landscape that was threatened. I felt it, as I felt so many things that first pandemic summer, as a devastating loss. As is typical of my climate grief, it set my climate rage to burning.

* * *

In her 1998 book, *All My Rivers Are Gone*, Katie Lee, the bawdy folk singer/river rat/activist, details her ultimately unsuccessful efforts to block the construction of the Glen Canyon Dam on the Colorado River, which created Lake Powell. Lee fell in love with Glen Canyon on a series of boat trips she took down the river starting in 1953, and, convinced that anyone who saw the beauty of the canyon for themselves would be against drowning it under a reservoir, her first efforts to protect it centered around sharing it. She wrote and performed songs about the beauty of the river and the canyons, invited friends to join her on her adventures through it, much in the same way I led my kids up mountain summits, the same way I take everyone who visits me to Rocky Mountain National Park. I share Lee's belief that the more people fall in love with open, wild spaces, the more people will fight to save them. Ideally, anyway. In 2020, the governor of Colorado issued "Safer at Home or in the Vast Great Outdoors" orders for COVID safety, which led to a 23% increase in visitation to state parks and almost certainly at least that much in the backcountry, where such statistics can't be reliably collected. Many areas saw double or triple their normal amount of use, and not everyone was well-behaved. Volunteers and rangers reported increased vandalism, overwhelming amounts of human and pet waste left in the backcountry, and illegal fires. Lee came to call this problem the ecological Catch-22. "Saving a wilderness," she wrote, "takes enough people to ultimately ruin it."

* * *

At least four of Colorado's 2020 fires, Cameron Peak, East Troublesome, Grizzly Creek, and Williams Fork, were almost certainly human-caused, and my anger about this specific carelessness has merged with the permanent dark ball of rage I carry in my chest about our society's overall lack of care—for climate, for human diversity and biodiversity, for, as the pandemic revealed, life generally. Of course, sometimes you can get away with it. Not every campfire becomes a wildfire, and I'm sure that must be the reason some people won't stop lighting them, despite fire bans and air quality alerts and all our recent lived experience with devastating fires.

I don't know how to share the wilderness with people who can watch a fire burn over 200,000 acres, burn 224 homes down to ash, and still insist on some sort of "right" to light a campfire any more than I know how to share the planet with climate deniers. I certainly don't know how to answer the pointed, accusatory questions my teenagers have for me about how we let the world get to this point. Their climate grief, like mine, also morphs into rage, but they have cultivated a sort of resigned pessimism about their future. They approach their climate activism and advocacy with a grim sort of fatalism, an awareness that their efforts, while essential, may not change anything. This too is a source of grief and rage, that I can't assure them otherwise, that I am no comfort at all.

* * *

I was 23 years old when *All My Rivers Are Gone* was published, and when I read it for the first time, just a few years ago, I wondered who I might have been if I'd read it sooner, if I'd carried Lee's fierce voice with me all this time. Lee was most joyful in nature when she could experience it "free, bare, naked, *tout ensemble*, buckass, nude, birthday-suited, in the altogether." In a photo taken in 1957 titled 'The Pagan,' she stands back to the camera, naked, surrounded by sandstone walls so varied and beautiful the color changes are obvious even in black and white. I recognize Lee's sense of ease in that space, her sense of communion, her sense of celebration—I experience nature this way too, and I want these experiences to be available for everyone.

By 1963, though, the Glen Canyon Dam was built, the diversion tunnels closed, and Glen Canyon, inundated, was becoming Lake Powell. Lee went back in a boat she named *Screwdriver*, or *Screwd river*, and for the next few years, she mourned the places she had explored and loved, serving as a witness as they disappeared underwater. When asked if it wasn't a form of torture to watch the canyon disappear, Lee responded: "Do we leave the bedside of our loved ones while they're dying? No. Most of us watch over…until they go. And when they're gone, we grieve—grieve long and deep…"

* * *

Just before the biggest fires erupted in 2020, my father died of cancer. We nursed him at home with masks on. As he grew weaker, my children helped us transfer him from wheelchair to bed and back again, in and out of the car, to and from the toilet. We were in the room when he passed, heard the ragged cadence of his breathing change, then stop. It was peaceful. We held his funeral online.

What I know to do with my grief is rub nature all over it, wait for solace to soak in, so a week later, my husband and I went on an eleven-mile trail run through Bobcat Ridge Open Space. The sky was hazy with smoke from earlier fires, which hadn't yet begun to drop ash, like rain, over hundreds of miles of land, hadn't yet tinted the bright blue summer sky to the smoke-fueled yellow-pink hue it carried for much of August. The trail, with its ankle-breaking rocks and ample rattlesnake habitat, required vigilance. The scar of a years-old fire had left it unshaded save for a lovely wooded section on the far end of the loop. Even in the arid interface between the short-grass prairie and the foothills of the Rocky Mountains, there are slopes like this that hold moisture longer, where trees and shrubs filter and modulate the relentless summer heat, and they feel as rare and necessary as oases in the desert. We stopped to rest in the cool shade, and once I started weeping I couldn't stop. My father, who used a wheelchair, could not access this place while he was alive, and I realized in that moment that he would never see it.

Months later, the Cameron Peak Fire reached Bobcat Ridge and burnt through those patches of haven forest, and I felt certain I'd never see them again either. The trails were closed until further notice. Scientists are discovering that increased heat and drought, driven by climate change, are preventing some of Colorado's forest species from recovering after intense fires like these, that they don't always grow back the same way they grew before.

* * *

In April of 2022, the Department of the Interior announced that they would reduce the amount of water delivered to California, Nevada, and Arizona in an emergency effort to keep Lake Powell from dropping below the levels necessary for the Glen Canyon Dam to produce hydroelectric power. Climate change in the region will cause even hotter temperatures, even less precipitation. We are most likely experiencing permanent aridification, not a temporary drought. Most available science predicts that the water will deadpool behind the dam as early as next year. Or, as Katie Lee would almost certainly see it, we killed that canyon for nothing.

My oldest child, now a college sophomore, studies Ecology and Sustainability and Geographic Information Systems. She texts me screen shots of the maps she creates, maps that show where American beaver habitat might support Gunnison sage-grouse recovery, maps that show the distance between her college campus and local outdoor recreation areas, maps she hopes might one day reveal climate solutions, paths that lessen human impact on the environment. For her 20th birthday, somehow only months away, I'm gifting her Lee's book. The fires have already destroyed many of the places I taught my daughter to love, and as the climate catastrophe shapes the trajectory of her life, I worry that she will lose many of the things she fights hard to save. In the face of this hard and enraging truth, I hope she can find moments in nature, as Katie Lee did, "…when I didn't have one minute of anxiety or trepidation, didn't do or say a single thing that didn't come naturally. No holding back, no showing off…feeling the right and wrong pressure, the angle and balance with the balls of my feet, letting intuition tell me where solid footing is." I hope Katie Lee will help her remember that the fight is always worth it.

* * *

Even after these years of losses, even facing a future of climate losses, I am, by nature, in nature, a hopeful person. And there are reasons for hope. Land managers are listening to indigenous methods of forest management and fire suppression. The water crisis in the West is forcing compromise and creativity that may well lead to meaningful conservation. The trails and wildernesses I love are still full to bursting with humans who feel…I don't know how they feel, exactly, but I hope it's a sense of ease, of communion, of celebration. Katie Lee, despite all her misgivings, concludes her book about the pain of losing Glen Canyon by sending readers into nature to find a place they themselves can love as deeply:

> "Let me urge you (no matter the odds) to seek out such a place. Why? Because you *need* it, whether you know it or not. If and when you find it, tell no one else where it is. Keep it as long as possible, and, like a loved one, cherish it, being aware that love is also pain, discovery, joy unrealized, and—sooner or later— loss."

The trails at Bobcat Ridge re-opened, and on Thanksgiving Day 2021, we ran that same eleven-mile loop into the forested grove where I'd grieved my father. The low bark of the ponderosa pines was blackened where fire scorched them, but it did not burn past that outer layer, had not damaged the heart wood. Those trees are still alive, as are the Rocky Mountain maples we thought we'd lost forever, which seem to have been spared completely. Cloven tracks in the trail mud indicated a herd of elk had been through the area, as had a large bobcat (or a small mountain lion). As we rested among all this resilience and strength and grace, my grief and my rage regulated themselves, my fear became muted as my breathing slowed. I cried under those ponderosas that day, too, for everything they'd managed to survive, tears of gratitude as well as grief.

Despite Katie Lee's warning, I have told you where my cherished place is. I am inviting you to find it, hoping you will love it as deeply as I do, because keeping it a secret won't keep it safe. Like every other beautiful place on this earth, we already share it. We are, all of us, already making our own weather, and we have choices, and there is still time.

The Recycling at Isaiah Gardens

Carolyn Ferrell

Do not. *Do not*, I repeat, throw trash in the cans in front of Building #3. Look at your hands. If you see you got diapers in them, or orange peels, pizza crusts, bobby pins, cigarettes, hair—well, *that* goes down your floor's trash chute. The one in your hallway marked DEPOSIT TRASH HERE NYCDSPW. The cans in front of Building #3 are for Paper and Cans and Bottles. Nothing else, especially not paperwork. DO NOT throw your paperwork into those cans bins. Keep your paperwork with you AT ALL TIMES. Because it could be you think THE AUTHORITIES are coming to check the building out when in reality they coming to check *you* out. Be aware—the NYC Department of Sanitation and Planetary Welfare don't play no games.

Do not spy. I *repeat*. Do not spy or repeat stories on neighbors *in the name of climate changeability*. That means you Miss Fields of 5G. Miss Sharpe of 2G don't have nothing to do with you or your Paper or Cans or Bottles. She ALSO don't want to know how your husband really died and if you cashed in his policy behind everybody's back to buy you a new Buick. She don't care if you order biscuits from Sylvia's down in Harlem once a week per delivery instead of making them by hand like the rest of us mortals. Put down your periscope, Miss Fields of 5G. Miss Sharpe of 2G don't have time for you seeing as how busy she is crocheting that afghan with the Sprockets from Immaculate

Conception Junior High (it isn't particularly my taste but who died and left me judge? I just know I wouldn't want an afghan on my bed that said *SAVE THE WORLD GODDAMMIT* in cute pink yarn). Just mind your sustainable beeswax. Any further problems please call Keesha at the NYC Department of Community Climate Peace, ext. 2499. Keesha will have the answers.

It's what the fancy places like Riverdale or Kingsbridge have been doing for some time now. (*Years?* OK then, they been doing it for *years*): recycling. Separating the dead from the living, the *good-for-the-planet* from the *going-to-hell-in-a-handbasket-for-the-planet*. One day THE AUTHORITIES handed out documents entitled the Better World Directive and next thing you knew, we had to look at our garbage with kindly eyes. We had to talk to our garbage in sweet voices, we had to let it know that it was part of something larger than all of Isaiah Gardens. We had to prepare for "Inspection." Everyone in Buildings #1 through #10 sort of agreed *why the hell not* except for those oldsters at the Senior Center in Building #8, serious as the grave, no pun intended. They were pure against "Inspection." Because since when is garbage more important than people? they asked. Since when do THE AUTHORITIES care more about filth and scum than the sanctity of human life, us *ladies and gentlemen* up here suffering, no heat or hot water for three days straight, then the grandkids don't call us *ever* seems and on top of that, someone's speakers out the window that WILL NOT STOP PLAYING "Going Up Yonder?" We're not nobody's slaves, the Senior Center says (somewhat incongruously, I might add, given their *elderliness*)—but of course THE AUTHORITIES don't want to hear any of that, and I'm also inclined to view those ramblings as nonsense. Not everything has to go back to slavery days, just saying.

Try to remember. All I'm asking is that you try to remember. When you see these big blue bins in front of Buildings #3, #5, #7, and #10, please sort things out. Do not. *Do not*, I repeat, fill them with: leftover pie crusts, Three Musketeers wrappers, torn shopping bags from Century 21 or Food Bazaar, fake nails. Do not throw your bones, chicken or otherwise, into those ~~bins~~ receptacles. We are not slavery, we are not downtrodden. We can, in fact, be like those fancy places, Riverdale or Kingsbridge—even our neighbors (sort of) in Co-op City. Be aware! We CAN know the difference between crumpled corn muffin wrappers from Isaiah Gardens Deli versus the crumpled forms you needed to fill out last week for the foster care program but you forgot and now it's maybe too damn late seeing as how the deadline's passed and why in the world did you ever think someone would want to look you in the eyes and say, *Mom?*

Buildings #4 and #6 get their Paper and Cans and Bottles carted away in special yellow and black striped receptacles every Wednesday. The rest of the Buildings have to alternate between weeks, like the rest of the Bronx. Buildings #4 and #6 may go about putting on airs like they are the darlings of the NYC Department of Terrestrial Terror and Environmental Misbehavior, but we know the truth. Those people over there just plain nasty.

In the beginning, Building #2 was the start of everything ecological. That's where most of the Immaculate Conception Sprockets live, a.k.a. the youth of Isaiah Gardens, a.k.a the action-packed hope of our corner of the Bronx: Sammy Abani, Joseline Diaz-Hunter, Callie Brown, Bellerina and Angelina Fromm, Malik Wiseman, Cody Collins, the list goes on. The Sprockets—so called because they set everything in motion, as in: *you can teach an old dog new tricks*—they were the first to go door-to-door handing out *revised* copies of the Better World Directive (*viz*: the Better World Directive 2). They were the first to tell the residents that there was such a thing as light pollution; they were the first to tell the seniors in Building #8 not to wear fur. If I had kids I would want them to look and act like the Isaiah Garden Sprockets. If I had kids, and they were over at Immaculate Conception, bored out of their gourds and feeling sad about being PART OF THE PROBLEM while some crusty old nun shows them a ~~filmstrip~~ video of our poor earth and mentions how we are ALL killing it softly (*"I brought you into a fertile land to eat its fruit and rich produce but you came and defiled my land"*)—my kids, my very own Sprockets, would stand tall and say *we need to be doing something about our environmental obnoxiousness or else we'll ALL be going to hell in a handbasket, every last one of us, no matter White nor Black, rich nor housing projects*; and if that cruciferous clergywoman says something like, *Children don't cry, the Lord will protect, the Lord will instruct,* my very own Sprockets will reply: *Sister, it's really up to us. WE ARE THE SOLUTION.*

(The foster care paperwork is sitting right on my dearly departed gran's coffee table. There's not a stain upon them, save for the crumpling and the weird oniony splotch from who-knows-where? Who or what can I be? Will someone ever want to say *Mom?*)

In the past, the Sprockets who reside in Isaiah Gardens *most definitely* have brought their school knowledge home to their parents—which, in Building #2, happens to consist of a lot of nursing, pre-school, and union-jobbers. Smart folks, in other words—*edumacated*, as Keesha sometimes softly jokes. Those folks likely heard their kids out (unlike the parental units in Buildings #9 and #10 that only use their babies to find the TV remote) and said: Thank you for reminding us to do the right thing. We love you babies. We want our Mother Earth to win. We couldn't be prouder. (Sadly most of these Sprockets are getting ready to graduate now and head out for the greener pastures of Bronx Science or Horace Mann and leave us mortals back here in the trenches. In the words of the philosopher R. Nevil: *C'est la vie*.)

Do not be afraid.

Do not be afraid to call Keesha. She will answer the phone like "This is Miss Dabney of the NYCDCCP what is your concern?" but don't let that put you off. She *is* and *is not* one of THE AUTHORITIES. She will always ask for your ID and tell you that you are LATE AGAIN but then she will stick up for you—as in, *she will* look NYCDHPSSS (the New York City Department of Housing Project Sustainability and Spartan Spirit) in the face during the PSI (Preliminary Surprise Inspection) and ask why do they have to treat Isaiah Gardens like they're the enemy? Isaiah Gardens has JUST as much sense as those buildings in Riverdale and Kingsbridge—maybe even more! There are lackadaisical people in the world and there are goodhearted people in the world and Isaiah Gardens happen to be in the latter category. Before doing a three-snap Keesha will say: Don't underestimate them, NYCDHPSSS! Isaiah Gardens is a force to be reckoned with, believe you me! Bring on your watch dogs—they ain't afraid!

("Inspection" being no joke. First Post-Preliminary happening tomorrow and damned if I want Keesha looking like she's got Alpo on her face.)

Because Keesha is also a force. There was that time some months ago when she asked me why I didn't have any kids because the way I looked out for Isaiah Gardens made it clear I had a natural maternal instinct. When I was quiet, she lowered her eyes and begged my forgiveness for asking something so thoughtless. *Not everyone needs kids to be a mother,* she said, *That's all what I was meaning.* I told Keesha I wasn't offended. I told her my life, in fact, never seemed to have much time for kids, what with thirty years plus pension from the NYC Department of Elder Lovability and Microclimate Management, then no partner whatsoever with the hours I kept. Then moving in to take care of my gran in Building #10, then winding up staying here at Isaiah Gardens, where I have dutifully checked every inch and nook and cranny and no gang warfare whatsoever (thanks to me) and no drugs anywhere to be seen (double thanks to me); this has never been a paid position so clearly I do what I do out of love. *You are the heart and soul of these houses*, Keesha told me. *You're more than a mother. You're a goddess.* I blushed. That Keesha.

(She has brown eyes and brown hands that slip your paperwork back to you with the gentlest of ease. One time Keesha said to me: *I found these documents in the recycling receptacles, Ms. Willis. I can't imagine you would want them to go to waste. Please take them back.*)

Building #7 has a couple cerebral palsy kid-mothers in it, scooting their kids' wheelchairs past the ~~bins~~ receptacles in order to make those special schoolbuses, the short ones, you know which ones I'm talking about. I see those mothers wave their kids off, then try to put the cans and bottles and newspapers in the right places and I know they mean well even when it doesn't actually happen. No one will hold it against them. Those mothers will not cause the "Inspection" to fail, even if they sometimes place diapers and tissues in the openings meant for soda cans and toilet paper rolls and organic egg cartons. Their faces flush. Do I want a flushed face as well? (Am I worthy? *Mom.*) Building #9 has those so-called college students (and yes, Bronx Community does too count!) but as far as we can tell, saving the planet is not on the same level for them as littering the floors with protest posters while simultaneously leaving a trail of wings and Styrofoam containers from elevator to door, like those kids in *Hansel in Gretel*—what were their names again?). Damn.

Some of those posters say:

> CITY HALL SATURDAY 10:00 AM
> MOTHER EARTH MARCH FOR OUR GREEN!!!

or:

> COME THIS FRIDAY NIGHT 8PM
> DON'T LET THEM TAKE
> OUR GREEN FROM US!!
> ISAIAH GARDENS SENIOR CENTER BUILDING #8

or:

> ONLY YOU CAN PREVENT
> OUR GREEN FROM
> DISAPPEARING!

(Someone—maybe Miss Fields of 5G—keeps adding an S to the word GREEN. And I have to laugh, and if you honest, you have to laugh, too.)

Keesha was the one to come out and remove the vandalized posters. She looked me up and down—as if I could be capable of such ignominy— and said, *Ms. Willis, you know this ain't funny. This ain't right. If we don't lead our people the right way, who will?* Shaking her pretty little head. Sounding so sanctimonious that I wanted to shout, *We ain't in church, Keesha! No need to get all up in MY FACE when I wasn't the one who added that S!* And I wanted to shout that and perhaps I did, because Keesha suddenly put her soft brown hand on my arm and said, *Apollonia, I meant you no disrespect. I know you love Isaiah Gardens with your heart of hearts, and that you care about its future, and that you WILL HELP the residents understand the importance of saving our green.* And suddenly my heart is full and back to remembering things correctly, and I just wish all the time my gran had had a touch more faith in me. I want to kiss Keesha but it just winds up on her cheek. Here I was thinking she was the enemy. *My bad.* I apologized and all was forgiven.

Do not think of yourself as a victim. Even when the NYC Department of Sanitation and Planetary Welfare issued a follow-up to the Better World Directive 2 (*viz*: the Better World Directive 3) that began: PEOPLE! YOU CAN'T BE HAPPY IF YOU DON'T GOT A WORLD TO BE HAPPY IN! GET IT TOGETHER OR ELSE! DON'T SEND A BOY OR GIRL TO DO A MAN OR WOMAN'S WORK! RECYCLE GODDAMIT!

And as if on cue, one of the lazy fathers in Building #4 started walking up to everyone with a nuisance Bible talking about: *The earth is defiled by its people; they have disobeyed the laws, violated the statutes and broken the everlasting covenant.* Some told him to shut the hell up. Some told him to go home and put some clothes on. The Senior Center at Building #8 told him to come in and have some coffee but he refused so they told him forget you then, crazy old coot. Not last week when this man passed by me tending to the tulip bulbs outside of Building #7, he gave me this look. And even though the sun was shining directly in my eyes, I knew he knew. *He knew.* Where there is a will, there is a way— and maybe we all are onto something, each in our own, immaculate approaches.

Last week was also when Keesha made a surprise visit and looked everywhere. Again the sun was sparkling and the air was as crisp as snowdrop blossoms. She grabbed me by the arm (was I that lost in thought?) and smiled her usual luminosity. *Oh, Ms. Willis, these recycling containers are looking so much better! I know you trying, I know the Buildings are trying, and I appreciate it so very much! I appreciate you so very much, Ms. Willis! We will get there.* Of course, my heart flew out of my body and circled the ~~bins~~ containers the rest of the day—can a heart be a cherub as well as a goddess? I SO needed that luminosity! Because just last month the NYC Department of Elder Lovability and Microclimate Management had written me an answer on the flimsiest onion skin stationery:

> We're sorry, Miss Willis, but we are not in the position to offer a letter of recommendation to one of our former employees in regards to foster parenthood as it presents a conflict of interest pursuant to Employee Code 117 of the City Code 118 of the New York State Department of…etc., etc.

(The last line being: *You know, back then you were no angel.* In red magic marker no less!)

But when Keesha looked at me through the snowdrop air, I wanted to reach back in time and straighten my wrinkles and crow's feet and weird-working hips and shout, *Who the HELL are you AUTHORITIES calling no angel? Forget you to infinity and back!!! I'm better than you ALL DAY LONG.*

We all are better. We forget to remember that. *Don't forget.*

This morning Miss Fields of 5G beckons to me in the courtyard of Building #8. I can see a murmur of senior heads in the distance behind her, all gathered behind the door at the Senior Center, clucking and waiting and maybe a few pairs of hands folded upon stomachs. *Say Ms. Willis*, Miss Fields calls out. I am in the middle of my walk-through as Volunteer Buildings Coordinator (a fancy word THE AUTHORITIES gave me to check on things in my spare time which is all the time, unless a foster child shows up and makes me his or her own) and I stop in front of Miss Fields while she nods in that old courtly way the seniors do. *We been in there reading all them Better World Directives*, she whispers to me. *We been studying them, actually, Ms. Willis.*

I told her I'd only gotten up to the BWD3. *There's more? Won't you please elucidate, Miss Fields?*

She pointed her finger hither and thither.

The Better World Directive 4 appeared on all the front doors to the buildings in Isaiah Gardens:

> People! You can't keep throwing away all your trash like it's the
> same! Stop being   LAZY
>   MEAN
>   INCONSIDERATE
>   IRRESPONSIBLE!
> People! Put your Recyclables in the APPROPRIATE BINS!
> Violators will be fined, possible Rikers.
> WE WANT THE WORLD TO GO ON!
> THINK OF FUTURE GENERATIONS!
> DO NOT SEE THOSE GENERATIONS
> LOSE THEIR MOTHER EARTH.
> PEOPLE! Bring back the WILD INDIGO and the
> SWAMP SUNFLOWER!
> Don't let this be the end!!!
>   SIGNED the students of
>   P.S. 78 Anne Hutchinson, Grades 1 and 2

Miss Fields could have had tears in her eyes (who can tell when it comes to old people's rheum?) but then she unweepily whispered, *Why haven't we grown, Ms. Willis? These little kids up here* growner than us—*what happened, Miss Willis?* She waved her hands at the supermarket fliers stuck in the chain link fences around Buildings #9 and #10 of Isaiah Gardens: the craggy coffee cups, the puckered plastic milk gallons. *It didn't used to be like this when we first started*, Miss Fields said. *We were just inside telling each other about the old days, when people acted with respect. When people cared whether they lived in a pigsty or not. And those people were us, Miss Willis. What happened, Miss Willis? What happened? All we want to do is just sit back and cry!*

Do not just sit back and cry! I repeat: *do not just sit back and cry!*

(I had no idea whether Miss Fields of 5G was in favor of the <u>Better World Directives</u> or not. Did she think her and her aged cohort would perhaps be the ones carted off to prison? She walked back to the senior center doors, and again I could feel that gray-headed murmur of old folks eye me with judgment. But judgment about *what?*)

I sat down on the bench next to the PAPER ONLY ~~container receptacle~~ bin. In the old days we could blame everything on the Allerton Houses. (Yes, I'm looking at you Miss Harvey of 2B and Mr. Washington of 7R— you and your Allerton Houses cousins who frequent our buildings all the time and leave recyclable Seagrams bottles right on the footpaths!) I put my head in my hands and told myself, Please don't say you can't teach an old dog new tricks!

Do learn new tricks! I repeat: *there is enough love to go around for everyone.*

Last night I used the broad side of my hand and straightened out the crumpled paperwork for the foster care people. I could wax sentimental and say something like, The Future Is What You Make It. But isn't this the truth: that the future is the *present*, and the present was *yesterday*? Why do we put all our eggs in the future? Every damn thing is staring us right in the face.

Do not be afraid. Tomorrow is "Inspection." Tomorrow is just one in a series of many. We can walk or we can run.

Tomorrow I get up and the weather is summertime sunny. It is still March, though, and the proverbial winds have kicked up, though you wouldn't know it if you saw what I saw: Building #6 is neatly posted with mini posters, undisturbed by the gusts, that read, BLACK LIVES MATTER IN ALL WEATHER; Building #1 is neat as a pin, no loose hair curlers; and though Building #4 remains somewhat shabby and squall-blown (will we EVER have enough Food Bazaar sales fliers???), there are clear recycling bags nestled OUTSIDE their bins, which I take to mean that the bins are full up. It's happening. I see Miss Sharpe of 2G and Miss Fields of 5G walking next to each other towards the Youth Community Center in Building #4; they are not arm-in-arm (as you and I would've preferred to have seen) but they are also not squabbling. I don't see any Sprockets about, though I do see the cerebral palsy buses idling next to Building #7 (you don't need to remind me to tell them that idling is bad for our air—I'm already on it!). One of those cerebral palsy mothers is carrying a canvas tote with probably enough recyclable juice boxes to feed the world. Life is moving. Forwards, upwards, diagonal, circle back and up. What, in reality, is there to be afraid of?

It is tomorrow; and I plan to call Keesha over at the NYC Department of Community Climate Peace and thank her for saving those documents. I wonder how she would feel about getting a bouquet of thank-you wildflowers on her desk? Freshly picked from Community Garden #45, corner of Bouck and Gun Hill Road. Swamp pink and large-flowered trillium and marsh marigolds. One never knows until one does.

Tomorrow I pass that same father who spouted all those Biblical gales. He's got a yellowed Christian Science Monitor under his arm and a big smile upon his face. Still dressed in his bathrobe, but not as scary as before. *Good morning, Ms. Willis. Would you happen to know the time?*

My watch says it's just past school breakfast, I tell him, and he smiles even wider.

I brought you into a fertile land to eat its fruit and rich produce.

Much obliged, sir, I answer.

Thank you, he says. *Thank you, Ms. Willis. Thank you.* He makes a big show of throwing the newspaper into the correct bin. His smile is never-ending. He could be a ghost.

The biblical man enters Building #8 and then all is quiet. I feel like shouting. Maybe I do start shouting. But no one comes out, no one shouts at me: DO NOT SHOUT!

Not even you or your whole "Inspection" team, walking towards me in the pre-hot-lunch sun. Because you know, even without me telling you: we can be as good as Riverdale or Kingsbridge or Co-op City. (Woodlawn had better not turn their noses up at us—we left them in the dust long ago, no pun intended.) We here at Isaiah Gardens can reinvent the wheel—we can turn it into a goddamn flying carpet. Just go ask the Sprockets, go ask the seniors. Ask the mothers, ask the fathers! Be aware! Oh, you say you want specifics? Well then—ask Mr.

Leftenant and Mr. Baines of 6K, Building #1. No, don't even ask—just go and look!

Seasonal Affective Disorder

Marie Myung-Ok Lee

There's a certain smell I associate with fall, a crispness that carries melancholy. These fleeting whiffs emerge in the heat of August in flashes, like heat lightning, so quick you can't tell if it was an olfactory mirage. Sub-notes of grasses drying and going to seed. Of trees informed by the length of days, sending out the invisible signal to their leaves to withdraw the chlorophyll that will leave only color behind. In New York City, there's the subtle ganky tang of gingko nuts crushed underfoot. But the smell recalls the same memory: I am in sixth grade, getting my new school supplies ready, covering my books with brown bags from Red Owl.

My son was born in the winter of the new millennium, when a faction of people thought the changeover to "00" would cause planes to fall out of the sky, for clocks to stop. The clocks didn't stop, but the climate change—the threat of which fossil fuel harvesting corporations have known about since as early as 50 years ago and have done nothing but hide that information in order to pursue profits—accelerated. That bill is starting to come due. Everyone was on Twitter yesterday watching footage of a seaside house being washed away by a risen ocean. The news was careful to state not once but twice that the house was unoccupied. I.e., nothing to see here, no one was hurt. Again glossing over the fact a lot of us, the younger people disproportionately, are going to be hurt. Escaping climate change is not as easy as making sure you are not home when the sea comes for your house.

MOTHERS UNEARTHED

For my son, the fall doesn't have a consistent smell. Some days we have leaves falling and budding at the same time, confused crocuses poking up out of the humus.

* * *

Fall is considered to be the Korean nation's favorite season. This mad love for the season that twins beauty and death appeared back when I first ventured into learning my mother tongue via night classes at NYU. Our Korean 101 textbook read: "Of all the seasons, Koreans think fall is the most beautiful."

One hears this sentiment all the time in Korea. It was new to me to think of a country, a people, having a favorite season— melancholy as part of its beauty. In the west, we seek the positive emotion, we do all we can to avoid the negative, which is probably why it's easy to receive and absorb the comforting lies of climate change denial.

I was born in Hibbing, Minnesota, a town of around 16,000. Resource extraction is its primary industry. The town had already, however, depleted most of the iron mines while I was still a child. I would hear all the old miners complaining about China undercutting the market, while our in-class filmstrips showed that no, all the ore geologists thought was unlimited, had already been dynamited out of the ground. We were told of a time that scientists felt the huge, vast ocean could swallow up all the excess carbon we produced starting from the industrial revolution. But in this, too, humans are too good at exceeding expectations for environmental destruction.

* * *

Winter of course was the primary season for people in Hibbing. Bob Dylan, who also grew up in my town, marveled in his memoir at the length and breadth of the unrelenting cold, the unending blanket of white—to the point one would start to hallucinate. The smell of burning wood evokes atavistic relaxation at the thought of a warm orange light; other human bodies gathering, hands unfurling toward the warmth.

But I remember more a crystalline freshness, almost an absence of scent, but not quite. My spouse is always impressed when I open our NYC apartment's window and declare it will snow. It always does. I can smell the flurries in the air before the flakes fall. It's a certain humidity— subtler—that I can catch when it's about to fall from battleship-gray clouds.

As with climate change, with such an unrelenting season, the western approach was to ignore or obfuscate. The "cool" thing to do was to blast the heat in your car and wear shorts all winter long. I remember in elementary school my mother making me wear clunky snow boots and being ridiculed by the other children. I took ice skating lessons, where we were made to wear short little dresses, flesh colored tights. A sweater, or even mittens, would have been laughed at. I used to hate skating practice. I'm not sure why my mother was so insistent on me and my sister taking lessons. We even had to take them in the summer, where the indoor rink would be just as miserably cold.

* * *

In the West we tend to mark the change of the seasons by somewhat egotistical measurements. There's a feeling of indignance in the Winter Solstice, when the sun is the furthest away from us and that day is the shortest, compared to the summer when it's the closest.

In Korea, there are beautiful poetic signposts. Dae borum is the first Full Moon after The New Year. There is another notation for "Enter spring." Even Buddha's birthday, Seokga tansinil, occurs on day 8 of month 4 on the lunar calendar, which means April or May. Every full moon is the 15th of the lunar month; I was charmed while watching the popular translated K Drama, Hospital Playlist, when one of the characters, Songhwa, looks up and sees the full moon and says, "I didn't know it was the 15th!" in the same way we'd say, "I can't believe it's June already!" The seemingly less stable lunar calendar is logical and primary in Korea.

When I was living in Korea for a Fulbright and working at an unwed mothers' home, I participated in a kimjang, a late-autumn ritual of mass outdoor production of kimchi for winter. With an almost shamanistic determination that the weather was about to turn cold, intersecting with estimations of the cheapest price for Asian cabbage, one day or two or three are spent in different outdoor spaces. It's not all done on a specific day but is more like the intermittent synchrony of fireflies. You'll just know when it's time.

In Seoul or the countryside you'll see men hauling mountains of cabbage brought in by farmers' truckload, the women laughing and gossiping while carefully cleaning the cabbages and soaking them in brine, preparing the fillings over the hours it takes for the cabbage leaves to properly soften. There are special tubs the size of children's wading pools to clean the cabbage. In the Seoul alley where I lived, the aunties used clean trash cans.

The job I was given for the kimjang was to peel the ginger, probably because little could go wrong with that. Still, an impatient auntie was aghast at how my whittling technique was wasting so much flesh. She grabbed my paring knife and showed me how to hold it perpendicular in order to scrape off the barest micro-layer of ginger-skin, to dig out between the appendage-like knobs as meticulously as one might wash between a baby's fingers.

In America, access to ingredients has changed so much by modern technologies–we can get watermelon year round. In Korea, daily food life, such as the preparation of kimchi, has not changed all that much since the Joseon Dynasty. The only sign of modernization in this timeless ritual was the use of a hose to wash away the effluvia of red pepper, shrimp paste, garlic skins into the gutter. At the end, each of us were gifted plastic bags full of kimchi, the housewives transferred them to a traditional nut-brown clay onggi on their tiny city balconies to ferment.

Richer people have separate kimchi refrigerators that, like a wine cooler, keep it at a correct temperature: cold, but not freezing, not unlike the genius tradition of burying the onggi in the earth, which would also keep it at the right temperature, no matter the ambient temperature. The fermentation process preserves the vitamin C in the cabbage in storage, to nourish its eaters through a Korean winter, powered by winds from Siberia, just as long and as cold as anything in Hibbing.

My kimchi is salad-fresh but also funky with heaping scoops of salted shrimp, a bright red from the hot pepper. As my plastic bags ferment in my tiny office-tel one-room, it mellows into the kimchi I know. I eat heaps of it with rice, make a tofu stew when the weather turns cold. It's so good that it doesn't even last me to the sour phase when it's delightful for fried rice.

I praise the ingenuity of my ancestors, resetting my cultural frame, remembering how my father restrained himself from eating kimchi when he was working (which, as the lone anesthesiologist in an isolated town, was often). Most people in our small town did not know what tofu was, much less kimchi, but the few who knew of it did not make favorable faces. My mother wouldn't let us kids eat it, as she was worried about the smell and being bullied. The only other time I came across a reference to kimchi was when our babysitter was watching MASH, and the GIs saw some Koreans burying what was mistaken to be bombs in the ground, only for it to turn out to be even more dangerous in the western conception: smelly, funky kimchi.

* * *

The first signs of spring loosen the snow, the way the shortening days of fall loosen the leaves on the trees. We kids were delighted when spring really got going, the snowmelt would form miniature rivers and the smallest children tried to fish in these streams. We would build dams, sail paper boats, running along with them downhill. The other side was undeveloped "dumps" where wild prairie grass had somehow managed to grow, even though our hill was constructed from old iron mine tailings. Overturn a rock and you'd see not soil, but orange-red ore. Walking there would turn the soles of your sneakers a bright red. In the dumps, snowmelt pooled and formed temporary lakes.

I remember the delight when the first pussywillows appeared at the "lakes" fringed by cattails, those velvet hotdogs on sticks swaying in the wind. How, as the days lengthened, the soft fur of the pussywillows would give way to green knobs that would unfurl into leaves, the lakes grew smaller, the cattails would swell, like grandma's antique sofa busting out foam at the seams. The smell of late spring, the heaviness of pollen, the hints of a hot summer, would smell of sex and reproduction setting off a happy restlessness that was almost unbearable.

* * *

With the warming earth, I wonder how kimjang will be affected, the erratic highs and lows, instead of the gradual, predictable march to winter. Will that affect the growth of cabbage? Will the warming earth render this backup method of storage obsolete? Unlike Americans, who laugh away weather extremes by frying eggs on car hoods and tweeting about it, Koreans note the unmistakable patterns, the climb of the yearly records. On the Korean news I see anxious headlines, "Weather forecaster warns of disappearing spring and fall," i.e., the weather is very cold and very hot and nothing, really, in between. The emotion of these headlines, unlike anything I ever see in the US, also grips me with dread and grief for what is already irrevocably broken, and what is to come.

In the US, we don't seem to react to the consequences of our own human assault on the natural world. In the Pacific northwest, mussels boil alive in their own shells. In our Minnesota neighbor, Canada, 500 people died in a heat wave this past June. The first climate change illness lawsuit was filed by a woman whose health—asthma and other ailments—have been caused by this new, wrong climate. In Minneapolis, where my mother lives, the streets have often buckled with heat in the summer—but also, now, in the winter, with cold.

I think about my son, who has autism and intellectual disability. If you ask him, "today is Monday, what is tomorrow?" he'll pick one from the slot machine in his head. This, I get. The seven day week is a product of industrialization, the work week. I am realizing that the wonderful thing about Korea's reliance on natural cycles, like the doctors in my K drama, means that even the most western-seeming people still keep track of the Lunar calendar, which forces you to look up into the sky. There are also no "leftover" days, like Leap Year, which need to be jimmied back in. Days progress, each erasing the last, with no remainders—going forward yet also circling back with the seasons.

When I ask my son, born into the new century, what season it is, he guesses. I try to give him mnemonics: Fall is when the leaves *fall*. Yet, it's almost eighty degrees out, I am sweating in my office, and people outside walk by in sandals and shorts, a few in season-appropriate down jackets, but slung over their arms or unzipped. The leaves similarly seem to be hedging. Many decide not to leave the tree, until, instead of coloring, they just fall off green, in slightly rotten wads. What I thought was a massive color change on the mountains when I was in Aspen in September was actually a climate-change related fungal disease in pine trees that was turning the needles golden. The aspens were still green.

I think of the three years when my best friend was dying of cancer, how flying into Asheville was often stymied by various odd and extreme weather systems, how many texts I sent to her of weather delayed flight—how one day in late spring as I taught my class before heading to the airport, the clear afternoon suddenly darkened, the window we had wide open to the spring breezes suddenly filled with swirling drifts of snow, the students staring at my wheelie bag as if themselves wondering if I was going to make it, where I was going, as the wind screamed and the students struggled to shut the window.

When I went to Asheville for a last time for her memorial service, the road to the venue was dangerously, newly flooded, and I almost didn't make it.

* * *

I suspect my son's disinterest in the seasons is part of his intellectual disability. But also, like any neurotypical people his age and below, it is possible he doesn't have a concept of seasons.

A few years ago at my high school reunion, I wanted to talk about climate change with my classmates. Growing up, Hibbing often made the national news in winter with jolly weatherman Willard Scott oohing about the negative temperatures in "America's icebox." Now, Hibbing has once again gained fame as the epicenter of climate change, an avatar of a phenomenon the National Climate Assessment labels a "polar switch": colder areas warming even more quickly than warmer ones; our town experiences the largest temperature difference in warming temperatures over its 1906-1960 average.[1]

But classmates tell me to shut up, hurry and get drunk.

Now the seasons don't smell like seasons. When I take pandemic walks with my son to the Harlem piers, the tang of gingko is just as often the tang of an ominous rot odor emanating from the sewer grates, even in the middle of "winter" (the quotes marking that it's often 60-70 degrees). From time to time, it smells like monsoon season in Korea—but that also is not a smell of seasons, because Korea has monsoons, and New York City does not (or should not). But now we have climate change rains that seem like someone is pouring water straight from the sky from a huge bucket.

In fall, the leaves are never as crisp.

I want to make my son apple cider doughnuts but it's hard to get in the mood when I'm sweating.

---

1 Rising Temperatures (2014, May 7). *The New York Times.* https://www.nytimes.com/interactive/2014/05/06/us/Rising-Temperatures.html

MOTHERS UNEARTHED

My son often says, "It is Mommy's job to keep me safe."

I am deeply moved by this trust, I take it as an "I love you." He is dependent on me to protect him, and nothing makes me feel more helpless and sad than thinking of leaving him some day to this boiled-mussel hellscape. It's because of him that I won't stop talking about, reminding people what we've lost—with more to continue to lose.

As mothers we bring life into this world, but the even bigger question remains: what kind of life—and death—will we be consigning our children to, if we don't take action? If we don't try to reverse the very course we have set ourselves upon?

Water

Chika Unigwe

The day the baby arrived, it rained so hard the streets flooded and the taxi Mmuofunanya was riding in was stalled. Mmuofunanya had to transfer to a bus high enough not to be swept by the floods. It moved so slowly, picking its way through the road, gingerly like an ancient creature, the pregnant woman feared she would give birth in the back of a dirty bus which reeked of chicken poop and moimoi. And she would have, as she told anyone who attended to her in the hospital, because it wasn't even ten minutes after she was taken into the labor room that her baby made its appearance, wrinkly and red like chili pepper. Mmuofunanya's husband, Eze, was playing golf before the rain started and did not witness the birth of his child. By the time he arrived, his umbrella dripping with rain, the baby had been cleaned, dressed, named and was sleeping face up, her hands spread out like wings on each side of her head.

"You can't name a child by yourself, it's not how things are done," he told Mmuofunanya. He towered over the cot and smiled at his new baby.

Mmuofunanya ignored him and whispered over and over again, *Mmiri. Mmiri m. My own water.*

"And what a silly name," he said, picking up the remote control of the TV on the table between Mmuofunanya and Mmiri. "Who names a child water?"

Mmuofunanya didn't want the TV on but she said nothing. He flipped through channels and flopped into a chair. He mumbled something Mmuofunanya could not catch. Outside, the rain was still falling. The sound of the storm muffled his voice. Mmuofunanya imagined the rain flooding the hospital room and sweeping him out, yet somehow sparing herself and its namesake.

* * *

Mmuofunanya loved playing in the rain as a child. Running in the rain with her mouth open, tongue outstretched to catch the raindrops. Even now, when she dreamed of those days, waking with the smell of wet earth in her nose, she cried for that time now long gone.

Her parents had died the year she graduated from university. One weekend when Mmuofunanya was out of town, a bush burning opposite their house got out of hand. The fire service had no water to quench the fire. Mmuofunanya had heard on the news of the devastation but had not believed it until she returned to what remained of the home she had left only a few days before. Her parents had been playing Monopoly in the living room as she walked out.

For days after, Mmuofunanya wandered the city like a madwoman. Ify, her best friend from university, had trailed her through Enugu, begging her to come home, to take a shower, to return to life. Eventually, Ify had had enough and used policemen to bundle Mmuofunanya into a car and bring her back. She kept Mmuofunanya under lock and key and forced her to shower and eat.

"You smell like a sewer," she had said to Mmuofunanya. Later, when they spoke about this phase of her life, she told Mmuofunanya she was trying to shock her into wanting her old life back.

"That life is gone," Mmuofunanya had said, "the fire destroyed it." It was the same month that she met the man she would marry, Eze.

* * *

In the hospital room Eze looked put out.

Mmuofunanya opened her mouth to tell him to leave but the words stuck in her throat like dry yam. There was a tightness, stretched from her throat to her chest and she coughed to ease it. It didn't help. Mmiri was still sleeping and if Mmuofunanya concentrated, she could see the baby's little chest rise and fall, rise and fall, reminding her of the Guinea pig she had as a child.

One day, the carrot she was going to feed the Guinea pig slipped from her hand and landed on its head, knocking it out. Mmuofunanya spent hours on her knees praying for a miracle. She had a hand on the Guinea pig's chest and each time it rose, she shouted to her father—who had told her the animal was unlikely to make it—that it was still alive. The moment she stopped keeping vigil beside it, when she allowed her father to convince her to take a break for lunch, the animal had died. She was afraid now to look away from Mmiri. With every breath, she thought, She's alive. She made this whole human. She was proud. The baby, as perfect as Mmuofunanya had dreamed it would be.

Eze stood. "I'm hungry," he said. He drove straight from the club and he hadn't eaten. He sounded angry, as if he was blaming Mmuofunanya for choosing today of all days to give birth. Or maybe he was blaming the baby for coming ten days early and scuppering his plans. The rain wasn't letting up.

"Let me pop down to the restaurant. How long are they going to keep you here for?"

"Four days," Mmuofunanya said.

The doctor had told her she was free to go home; she had an uncomplicated delivery. She didn't even have to push for a long time. She mentally prepared for a more difficult time but the labor was short and Mmiri slipped out so quickly that the doctor joked that she had never met a baby so much in a hurry to make its entrance.

"You're in for a disappointment, little one," the doctor said, "our world isn't that great at all, you'll see." She then laughed at her own joke.

Mmuofunanya hadn't thought it particularly funny. What terrible first words for her child to hear. When the doctor placed her on Mmuofunanya's chest, Mmuofunanya whispered sweet things in her ears. Her daughter would have a life of softness.

She couldn't go home yet, she told the doctor. She didn't feel ready yet. Her head hurt. The doctor winked and smiled.

"Fine. I'll keep you here under observation for another three days and see how you feel then." Mmuofunanya forgave the doctor then.

The tightness in her chest eased once Eze left the room. Even Mmiri's eyes fluttered awake as if she'd been shutting them until her father left. Mmuofunanya sidled out of her bed and lifted her baby in one easy movement as if she'd always done this. Why had she been so worried about becoming a mother?

It was more about having a child with Eze. The first year, she knew marrying him was a mistake,but what could she do? She had no family. Eze wasn't a bad man. He gave in to his anger sometimes. "But what man doesn't?" Ify had asked her.

"You're lucky to be married," Ify said. Ify's second boyfriend was dragging his feet about marrying her, and Mmuofunanya's first boyfriend had made an honest woman of her within a year of meeting. "If you weren't my bestie, I'd be jealous. Eze is the real deal ooh. He's fine, he has a good job, he loves you. He doesn't hit you."

Mmuofunanya conceded, thinking of her father's anger. Her father could simmer and hurl words that made her mother disappear into her bedroom and cry. One day, her mother had told her that if not for Mmuofunanya, she would have left her father. "His words kill my spirit," her mother had said. Mmuofunanya, sixteen and wise, had told her mother that if she wanted to leave, she shouldn't use her daughter as an excuse.

Her impatience with her mother now embarrassed her. She looked at her Mmiri, and she understood how a child could tie a woman down.

Three weeks before she found out she was pregnant, she found a text message on Eze's phone from "Queen." Eze's phone was ringing while he was in the bathroom. Perhaps it was someone from his law firm.

When she raised it to answer, she saw multiple messages from "Queen". And so, she read the first and then the second and then the third and fourth.

The Queen was pregnant.

She missed Eze.

Why was he not responding?

Wasn't he excited about having a child with her?

And then: *Go to hell, Eze. I WILL have MY child. I don't fucking need you.*

Eze hadn't denied knowing Queen. Yes. He was sorry he hurt Mmuofunanya but why was she snooping anyway? Ijuta isi nkita, iwelu agba ya mee gini? She was the one he married . Queen meant nothing to him. Just a woman he was messing with. What did he care about her bastard child?

Mmuofunanya was her mother's daughter. She wasn't raised to shout. Or to demolish things. But she could not stay. So, she went to the bedroom and cried. And then she drove down to Ify's house. Ify said she could stay with her. Eze might be fine but he wasn't all that. And he might be wealthy but what was the use of all that money if he went around cheating on Mmuofunanya and getting other women pregnant.

"There might be a position opening up on my campus for another Composition 101 lecturer. You should apply."

Three weeks later, after days of vomiting every morning, Mmuofunanya did a pregnancy test and watched as two pink lines confirmed what her heart already knew from the first day she ran out of Ify's kitchen gagging because she couldn't suddenly stand the smell of okra. When Ify returned from work, Mmuofunanya showed her the test, the pink lines luminescent like led lights.

"This doesn't change anything," Mmuofunanya told Ify.

"You don't even have a job yet. Who will look after you and the baby?"

Mmuofunanya said she would find ways.

"Do you know how many women would pray to be in your position?" Ify had asked her then, rubbing the bunions on her toes she got home from walking to the private university on Independence Lay Out where she taught and earned barely enough to pay her rent. "If I found a man as wealthy as Eze, biko, I'd give up this sufferhead job."

As a wedding gift, Eze had given Mmuofunanya a Benz. A secondhand one, granted, but it still retained a smell of newness. He paid for her to take driving lessons. Her monthly stipend was three times what Ify earned teaching three days a week. Yes, back then she was lucky. But Queen changed everything. In the three weeks she was gone, Eze had only called her twice. Both times, she told him she was never returning to him.

"Go to Queen and go to hell," she said, hoping she didn't sound like one of those melodramatic Nollywood actors she and Eze mocked. How could she go to him now?

"Do you or do you not want the baby?" Ify asked.

Mmuofunanya said she did. It was early days, but she could swear she already felt the flutter of the baby against her womb.

"Then you have no choice," Ify said.

She would endure, like her mother.

* * *

Mmuofunanya thought back to the day she returned to her husband. How heavy her body had weighed on her, how heavy her heart was. "If I'm doing the right thing, why does it make me so sad?" she asked Ify over the phone that night.

"Just concentrate on the baby you're carrying," Ify told her. When Mmuofunanya complained that Eze never apologized for cheating on her, Ify wisely reminded her that Eze had taken her back. "What if he'd chosen Queen? Asked you to go back to where you were coming from? Our men can do that, you know." Mmuofunanya knew but the knowledge did not console her. "You have to try to forgive and forget. Forget especially."

Mmuofunanya tried.

All through the pregnancy, she craved pepper. It was as if the baby were sending her a signal. Mmuofunanya would grind pepper—hot tatashe—and mix it in yogurt or spread it across her toast for breakfast. For lunch, she would have jollof hot enough to burn a hole through the roof of her tongue. At night, she ate yam with palm oil thick with pepper. That was the only way the baby in her womb would settle. If she ate anything bland, any food not furious with pepper, the baby squirmed like a worm and Mmuofunanya could not rest. When she told her doctor, she told Mmuofunanya that maybe the baby could see things. Did Mmuofunanya have issues she was bottling up? The doctor smiled to let Mmuofunanya know she was joking but there was an earnestness to her tone that invited Mmuofunanya to open up. She'd already asked why Mmuofunanya's husband never came with her to her appointments.

"He's busy with work," Mmuofunanya said.

"This is the 21st century. No man can ever be too busy to fit in 45 minutes of a prenatal visit," the doctor had replied.

As the rain fell outside, Mmuofunanya cradled her daughter in her arms. She understood now what the doctor had tried to do. She washed Mmiri over and over in the doctor's words. She told her, "The world is a hard place but you will survive. You will be strong. And resilient." She tried not to cry. "You will enter doors fear didn't let me open."

On TV, someone on a panel explained how this year's rainy season had seen more rain than in previous years. They said something about climate change. Environmental responsibility. Mmuofunanya shook her head. She remembered a story from her childhood. Her grandfather—still alive and agile then—had visited the family from the village, complaining of heavy rains that ruined farms. Ala, the earth goddess, he said, must be furious because when she got angry, she tore into the earth with so much rain that nothing could take root.

"And who could blame her," he said, "no one respects the earth anymore."

MOTHERS UNEARTHED

Mmuofunanya began to remember it all. The fire that killed her parents. Droughts. Floods. Climate change. Eze and Queen.

She sat up in bed and bounced the baby on her knees impatiently. Mmiri looked at her and made a face as if to smile. Mmuofunanya smiled, and was still smiling when Eze waltzed back into the room, a toothpick between his teeth. Mmuofunanya stopped smiling. Anger like hot pepper invaded her body.

"You should go," she told Eze. She hated that her voice was shaking. "Mmiri and I, we don't want you. Not now. Not ever."

Eze smirked. He said something about not being in the mood for jokes. Then about her finding her own way home whenever she and the baby were released.

At first, Mmuofunanya could not tell the pounding of her heart apart from that of Eze's footsteps hitting the tiled floor of the hospital hallway as he walked off. If she ran after him, she could still pretend it was a joke. She could beg. She stood there in the doorway listening to the rain pattering on, Mmiri in her arms. Later, when asked, she would say the rain hypnotized her. She felt immortal, like a goddess. Ala, angry with mortals for making a mess of the world. She heard the whoosh of Ala's waters cleansing the earth, preparing it for a new, better life.

She held Mmiri close to her and whispered over and over again, *Mmiri, may we be fearless.*

She Doesn't Want to be Called a Human

Kianny N. Antigua

I must admit, I was incredibly selfish before I had my daughter. As many—too many other Dominican women and men—born and raised on the island, I didn't give a shit about the environment. Why? Nobody else did. The government didn't care. No one spoke about pollution, or waste; the word "contamination" was only used to refer to drinking water, and Haitians.

Then, Mía came. And the world suddenly was not only the place where we all live, but the land that would hold my child. It contained the air she was going to breathe, the water she was going to share with her loved ones.

And then Mía turned three, and began talking about the sea, and the number of plastic bottles and bags we, humans, throw there as if there were no creatures that could be harmed. And then she turned five and six, and all she talked about was how she wanted to live in the forest, with the trees, and her loyal friends the animals.

At six, poetry came; seven, she didn't want to be called a human.

Humans litter
they hunt just because

air pollution

light pollution

they destroy habitat for no reason at all
global warming
they throw so much garbage in the ocean
humans suck

These were her words.[1] She was enraged with our privilege and lack of consideration of other living creatures—I would listen from a little corner and be ashamed—and her complaints went on and on.

"Do people throw garbage on their own homes the way they throw it on the streets?"

"Why rich people don't make more machines that clean the oceans?"

"I don't need any more clothes, Mamá," she once told me, "I have enough. We are just making more garbage."

Now I think twice before buying a bottle of water, while the memories of the once affluent Río Jaya, back in San Francisco de Macorís—my hometown—drill holes in my conscience. I think twice before drinking

---

1   When I told Mía I wanted to quote her in something I was writing, she didn't like the idea of me talking about her "intimate" things; then she read this piece and she seemed pleased with the outcome. She added, "People should know about this and change, with or without children."

from a straw. Sitting in the Malecón, in Santo Domingo, is a more depressing thought than the dream of a returning emigrant—the water is no longer sky blue; the shores of my island are covered with garbage (unless the beach belongs to an international hotel, and then they make sure the beach is clean for the tourists to enjoy). Going to the supermarket without a tote and shopping fabric bags mortifies me as much as inserting a tampon in my vagina.

And she, my Mía, is so angry still, and the rolling in of her preteen-self reminds me of this, and her need for naming, and climbing and talking to trees remind me of this; and more than my daughter, she is the mother, the voice of reason. She understands Mother Earth. And Mother Earth is angry. Why wouldn't She be? With a womb full of evolved Homo Sapiens, capable of flying to the Moon and beyond, modern gods capable of communicating at the speed of light from one side of the globe to the other, but incapable of taking responsibility for neglecting and harming the only home we have.

Today my daughter is ten and, through her words, her poetry (her very political poetry), activism, and observations, she continues to teach me about anger and love: anger for what we fucking selfish humans have done to destroy this planet and our blindness and lack of desire for taking a step; and love for Rubie Catillac, our cat, our chickens, which I would not name at this time, Angus and Ottis—our neighbor's dogs—and every other animal[2] and plant alive. If it were for her, this house would look like Ace Ventura's.

---

2   The first children's book I published titled *Mía, Esteban and the New Words* (Alfaguara, 2014) was born after seeing little Mía hugging and kissing the stinkiest sheep we saw at a town fair.

I wish I could tell you that I have done more than writing a few children's stories about this topic, that I have a plan, beyond my still selfish conscience, on how to be of greater help; that my rage and my sacrifice can compare to those of my daughter, and so many other brilliant youngsters, but all I have to offer is this everlasting shame, this body and heart that will forever support my daughter's wrath—because I, and you, didn't care.

Prime Coats

Stacy Parker Le Melle

In 2006, I sat with the physician in my pickup truck in the Baton Rouge strip mall parking lot, outside of Ichiban Sushi where he suggested we meet. Dr. Ben deBoisblanc had served as Director of Critical Care Services at Charity Hospital in New Orleans during Hurricane Katrina and the levee failures, back when flood waters devastated some neighborhoods and not others, back when people drowned if they could not ax themselves to the roof. He served with other medical professionals in caring for patients during the hospital lockdown. He scrambled and hustled to get help for his patients when the cavalry was nowhere to be found. Dr. deBoisblanc and his Charity Hospital colleagues saved lives until FEMA evacuated the last patients seven days later. They saved lives despite losing electricity and water pressure during the brutal August heat, despite feeling forsaken in the midst of disaster.

Ben, as he asked me to call him, was slim, blond, and tanned, though he looked tired, as if Katrina were still happening. A year had passed, and Katrina was still happening to everyone in Gulf Coast locales impacted by the storm and the aftermath. The more I interviewed people for my "Katrina Experience" oral history project, work I began in Houston just days into the natural disaster and man-made humanitarian crisis, the more I witnessed what it took for survivors to recover and to reconstruct their lives. It would take years to do so, and so much would never be recovered. Ben looked as if he had finished another sleepless night on his boat, Creola. It's where he had chosen to stay the Saturday before Katrina's landfall. Ben woke early that night because the Lake Pontchartrain harbor master cut the electricity that powered Creola's air-conditioning. He told Ben he was headed out because the approaching storm appeared catastrophic.

Ben may have been tired that night of our first interview in 2006, just coming off of his shift at Our Lady of the Lakes Hospital in Baton Rouge, where he worked in his days of displacement, but he was patient as he waited for me to insert a fresh tape into my minicassette recorder. Ben had a seven-day story to tell. For over two hours in my pickup, he spoke nearly uninterrupted. The gray afternoon was soon lit by parking lot lights and glowing business signs. I met Ben again and he spoke for two hours more. He told me what happened when he, the only member of his family still in New Orleans, hunkered down at Charity Hospital. He told me what happened after the hospital lost power, how they made their way through black interior hallways, the walls dungeon-wet. He shared the tricks and jerry-rigs and old school skills they recovered to keep their critically-ill patients alive.

* * *

Dr. Ben deBoisblanc, *50, was the Director of Critical Care Services at Charity Hospital in New Orleans during Hurricane Katrina. This interview was conducted in two sessions outside Ichiban Sushi Restaurant in Baton Rouge in 2006. Interviews were either before or after his shift at the Our Lady of the Lake Hospital, where he worked post-Katrina.*

Sunday, August 28, 2005

I woke up early Sunday morning and went over how to prepare my boat. I started grabbing momentos. I wondered whether I was going to see my boat again. I knew what hurricanes had done in Florida and other places to marinas, so I grabbed up a few pictures of my kids.

I looked over and I saw a picture of my dad, standing next to his boat. My dad had been deceased for about twenty years. The only picture I had like it, from when he was a younger man. I was very fond of it. I said, "Oh, I've got to get that picture." I started to take it down. Then I said, "No, why am I taking this down?" I somehow reasoned that his spirit would watch over Creola. I left his picture there. I thought, hell, if the boat goes down, at least he would want to go down with the ship.

I arrived at Charity around 8 or 9 in the morning. Got my activation bracelet — a little bracelet that tells people you belong there. I went up to the ICU. We had been through this drill before. It turns out to be a party. People arrived with lots of food: chips and dips, hot dogs. We took over our call room, the little family area/waiting room. We put down air mattresses. The air conditioning was going. It was very comfortable.

I was there as the medical director. There was an attending physician there named Francesco Simeone. Francesco's job was to focus on taking care of the patients, so I brought some work with me to do. We were getting all the news broadcasts. Everything was "Non-stop Katrina bearing down on New Orleans."

We sent home a lot of family members who were staying in the hospital. Only one or two family members were allowed with each patient. We had toyed with the idea of closing down the hospital, but it had been a place of refuge for the city of New Orleans for so long that we didn't think we could close it down. They'd done a mandatory evacuation order, but you could just sense that there were maybe a hundred thousand people that could not, would not, evacuate. The Superdome was filling up. We didn't think we could close a hospital when there were so many people who might try to turn to the hospital as a place of sanctuary. Sunday evening was very routine. I did a little bit of preparation. Not a lot. Mostly watched newscasts and worked on my computer.

The rain started to come down. The wind started to blow. I went and lied down in our call room.

Monday, August 29, 2005

I remember waking up about midnight. The wind blew pretty hard and the windows started to rattle. I could feel the building shake — a big, massive, concrete building that had been a civil defense shelter during the Cold War.

From 1 a.m. to 3 a.m., we heard windows popping out of buildings and crashing to the ground. I couldn't go back to sleep. I couldn't tell where the windows were popping out of–our building, or the building next to us? I just knew that they were popping and crashing. It was all very exciting.

We first lost power right around daybreak. The emergency generators kicked on. For reasons I still don't understand, the power went out again on our side of the hospital. We were plunged into darkness. There were very few windows in the ICU. The flashlights popped out. We'd done this drill a hundred times so four people ran to the bedside of a patient, grabbed a bag (manual resuscitator) and started squeezing the bag. We had about 11 patients in the Medical ICU. Nine of them were on breathing machines, mechanical ventilators — all of them very sick. Each person would grab a bag. I went around and I checked with each one. I went from bed to bed to bed, checking to make sure everybody was OK.

I remember getting around to bed 11, to check on a patient, initials HR. HR, this 23-year-old kid, he had Goodpasture syndrome. Goodpasture syndrome is a disease that causes you to have hemorrhaging in your lungs and kidney failure. He was sent to us maybe 2 or 3 days before the hurricane, from a small hospital in Independence. They sent him to us because we're an academic medical center. HR was on a ventilator, a breathing machine with a tube down his throat, on a very high oxygen concentration because of his lung failure. His respiratory failure was very severe. He was also getting dialysis.

There was a woman, CW, who was a respiratory therapist helping HR. I said, "CW, are you OK?" "Yeah, yeah, yeah. Fine." I left. Came back about twenty minutes later: "Are you OK, are you OK?" "Yeah yeah yeah." I insisted: "Why don't you let me give you a break? " She refused: "No, I'm fine. Alright. Came back an hour later. Got up to HR's room and I said, "CW, you're still here? Why don't you take a break? Let me give you a break." "*No, I'm OK.*"

It kind of gave me a little chill. I realized, *whoa*, CW wasn't going to let anyone mess with HR. That was her patient. I didn't realize it at the time, but I really think that it had something to do with the fact that CW was a single mom. Her only son, her everything, C, had died the year before. Sudden cardiac death, during football practice. Very sad. She was devastated by that. Took a long time before she could come back to work. This was a chance for her to feel like a mother again. A protector. No one, me included, was going to get in the way of that. I think it was people taking ownership for individual patients was why we did as well as we did.

The eyewall of the hurricane passed the hospital probably 8 a.m. The building shook in the face of the wind. The windows rattled. The windows above us blew out. The rain poured in. The rain water soaked down to the acoustic ceiling tiles. The tiles saturated like wet sponges. They started falling off the ceiling, right on top of the patients. The light fixtures fell out of the ceiling. It was a very exciting time. We were in the dark. The electricity had gone out. So Monday morning was just an adrenaline rush. We could see outside signs and trees being blown down. Just the ferocity of it all.

The rest of Monday was a struggle to keep patients alive. Most of the equipment in the ICU continued to operate, although it was alarming that it was on battery backup. We bagged the patients — actually squeezing the bags — because the ventilators were not happy very long on battery backup. We could see on the other side of the hospital that there was still electricity. Our side was black.

A few of our residents found some extension cords and strung together 300 feet. We plugged eight ventilators into this, using surge protectors and all these little multi-port extension cords. We stretched it as far as we could toward the other side of the hospital. It's a huge hospital. We got to the middle; we couldn't quite get to the other side. We plugged in to the only outlet that we could reach with our extension cords that had electricity: the Coke machine. We were able to power up a few of our ventilators that way and get back into business.

We had about an inch of water in the ICU. We started to clean up. Mopping up an ICU with an inch of water is a big deal, so we said, gosh, wouldn't it be nice to have a wet vac. We called our housekeepers, and they brought over a wet vac. They started wet vacc'ing up. Well, they had a long extension on the wet vac, and started in the central hallway, and started moving toward the ICU, cleaning up the water. At about 2 p.m., the power went out for our ventilators. The extension cord power went out–only to find out that the janitors had unplugged our extension cord to plug in a wet vac, not realizing what it went to.

We plugged back in. We had power via that extension cord for most of the day.

We did have small portable generators that were kept in the storage facility at the hospital, but they did not have fuel. The fuel was not stored on site. So we had these emergency generators in boxes that were totally useless. They were sitting in the hallway. We had plans, if we had had fuel, to bring them out to the fire escape and fire them up, and we could have plugged our extension cords in there instead of running all the way across the hospital. But we weren't too worried about it at the time. We did have this one outlet that was working more often than not.

The patients were doing OK. We experimented with different types of artificial ventilators. Some of them were gas-driven. Gas-driven works on a compressed oxygen source. We had oxygen stored in liquid oxygen cylinders. That continued to work throughout Katrina. The actual compressed air requires a compressor. That failed when the electricity went out. As long as we still had power on the other side, most things seemed to work. The suctions still seemed to work.

MOTHERS UNEARTHED

By Monday afternoon, the telephone service grew weak. The cell networks were overloaded. They were still working, but it was hard to get an outside line. You got a busy signal all the time. The water pressure was still on, but it grew weak as well. Systems were starting to fail.

Monday was so adrenaline-filled that when the wind started to die down, we started high-fiving each other. We just survived something really bad. The streets were dry. We thought we'd be going home Tuesday morning. We still had our extension cords plugged in, just kind of powering up our side of the hospital.

Monday night, the power went out again. We chased the extension cord — it was still plugged in, and we realized that the power was out in the whole hospital. We didn't realize then what had happened. As the sun came up Tuesday morning, we realized that the city was flooding from every direction. That's when the story really begins.

* * *

Ben told me this story in my truck. Before, New Orleans evacuee Printiss told me his story in a Houston park outside of the George R. Brown Convention Center. Others would speak to me on front porches, in living rooms, in restaurants throughout Texas, Louisiana, Mississippi and beyond. I was not a journalist, but I was a listener and a writer.

I was also a Black woman who felt sickened and shamed to see survivors left to fend for themselves, treated as threats. I found myself pushed and I actively pushed myself to get survivor stories recorded. Inspired by writer Studs Terkel's oral history work and playwright Anna Deveare Smith's interview-based theater performances, I gently shaped transcripts into oral history essays to share with anyone who wanted to know what it was like to be a survivor or to come to their need.

I did this to build understanding and empathy. To let people know that this could be them, and what to expect. To help the fearful see the humanity of each person impacted, so that maybe, next time, fear would not play such a central role in our response to catastrophes destined to repeat themselves as our climate crisis intensifies.

Now I am writing a book for my son, to help him understand what I learned from this experience and how it taught me that we cannot look away from crises in society.

But on August 29, 2005, the day Hurricane Katrina struck Louisiana, Mississippi, and Alabama, I lived in Houston, Texas. I taught creative writing to elementary school children and my residencies would not start until later in September. I was not yet a mother. I had time to watch news coverage for hours. Spellbound, I sat on my living room floor and switched channels between CNN and other major networks. They all reported live from New Orleans.

A Million Mouths Formed the Same Question

On Monday morning I watched live feeds from the French Quarter and the Central Business District. Broadcast journalists reported that New Orleans dodged a bullet. The high-rises lost windows, but look here — pavement, wet, but no standing water. No apocalypse. Only debris.

Only once before had I visited New Orleans. I knew enough to know that the national news correspondents stood on high ground. Why not take their cameras elsewhere?

I waited for the gravitas of the evening anchors, the comfort of Aaron Brown on his CNN show *NewsNight*. What is dread but brackish water rising inside us? Alone in the Houston apartment I shared with my first husband, K, I grew more anxious, certain that the cameras were tethered to safety. That what lay beyond…

Hours later CNN broadcast veteran journalist Jeanne Meserve reporting live from New Orleans. No video—we heard her voice on the phone. Finally, I thought. Someone left the high ground. On a boat. With a cameraman and his broken ankle. They traveled past the French Quarter and finally reported what so many of us feared. Meserve softly told of the screams. Of the pleadings. Of the calls for help from those huddled in their attics. Waiting. Praying and crying.

A million mouths formed the same question: Where was the help?

1-800-HELP-NOW

"The Red Cross needs our help. I urge our fellow citizens to contribute."
- President George W. Bush, August 31, 2005

Donate some money and you're done. Is that true? I wanted it to be true. If I wrote the modest check I could afford, I could watch the news and not cry as hard, for I did what I could do.

Problem one: I had little cash. Problem two: I wouldn't be done. But what could I do?

Everyone has limits. Mine was our apartment. K and I lived in a two-bedroom new construction apartment house north of Montrose near the Heights. One bedroom for sleeping, one bedroom for shared workspace. Our office overflowed with books, papers, and K's sculptures-in-progress, with walls thinner than the walls I complained about growing up when I played the radio every night so I wouldn't hear my stepfather snoring.

Thin walls. Paper wall thin. There might as well be no walls.

Houston is a six-hour interstate drive from New Orleans, a city very much connected to Louisiana by families that for generations migrated to Texas for work, with extended families working and living along the I-10 corridor. Once people in harm's way knew how catastrophic Katrina could be, many evacuated to Houston on their own, rented hotel rooms, or stayed with family and friends.

Then came the storm. Then came the levee breaches. Then came the catastrophic flooding of an American city at a scale we'd never seen before. That's when so many Houstonians blew my mind. They opened their homes to strangers. Single women adopted single mothers. Whole families adopted whole families. They gave them their spare bedrooms, living room couches. They gave more if they had it, or they shared what they had even if it wasn't that much.

What did I say? No. Not that. Our apartment was too small, I said. I don't know if I even brought up the question with K because the answer was so firm in my mind.

I once read that Americans do not sacrifice. They give of the surplus. Is that true, though? Maybe the writer didn't talk to enough Americans to know. But maybe the writer meant me. That I didn't sacrifice. When was the last time I gave up something I needed?

When I read about a clothing drive, K and I went to Target. We agreed to twenty dollars. We bought men's and women's underwear, and a baby's blanket. I wished we could have bought more, but we were in credit card debt as it was. There had to be limits.

Right?

That Feeling in the Air

Dread, but a flood of it. All over Houston. In my heart and in my stomach. The earth broke open six hours away and the wettest hell on earth was so close and here we were, getting espressos and breakfast tacos and living in air conditioning yet also living in this weather that rolled into our region that was not weather but dread from the millions of lives impacted from here to there and the emotions released, many of us hurt, many of us trying to help, trying to count our blessings but that dread was as real as any humidity, as real as anything saturating the swamp air in August.

At the Red Cross

Buses of evacuees arrived in Houston that Friday night, four days after the hurricane's landfall and the subsequent levee failures in New Orleans. The news said they came from the Superdome. I was so proud of our Houston Mayor Bill White who said we would help with open arms, not reluctance, and that we would *not* be a city that barricaded highway exits to block evacuee buses or gave them city jail cells as emergency housing. The city–in partnership with corporate, church, and nonprofit leaders, staff, and volunteers–would show survivors compassion and care. And that was final.

Saturday morning came and I wanted to volunteer at the Astrodome. I assumed I had to go through the Red Cross to do this, so I drove down to the Houston chapter offices.

I signed in, affixed my nametag. Two seconds later I'm commandeered to the phone bank. Now. No matter that this is my first time at the Red Cross, *ever*. I would be their voice.

They led a group of us to a cramped square room, the air dense with fatigue and anxiety. We waited for instructions near a long table filled with donuts and chips. Up in the corner, a TV played, the volume loud. A shot of buses arriving a few miles away. Someone began reciting a litany of things to know, pointing to a whiteboard.

That was part one of orientation. They walked us again, now, to a second building tucked behind the first. Up to the second floor. Not the third—that's where management lived. We were to stay on the second. In an expansive space three times the size of the "normal" phonebank, tables lined the walls. On each table were phones that never stopped ringing unless you left them off the hook.

A supervisor sat at the table near the elevator. So much ringing. Talking, but hushed tones. Volunteers, from age 18 to 70. Men and women. Different races, shades of skin. Again, that same tense air, same anxious mission. No TV played here. An older white man talked as a circle of other phone bankers formed around him. They all had urgent questions. He was busy explaining something. Wait. I'm confused. Was he talking about fishing? He looked and sounded like Cliff on Cheers. Someone said he's a volunteer as well.

The supervisor identified himself. He showed us phone numbers on whiteboards, handed us Xeroxed info sheets. But mostly, information came from the whiteboards:

Want to donate? 1-800-HELP NOW / Church Shelters (713) 313-5231 / Wal-Mart Connection: 1-800-236-2875 Option #9 / www.familylinks.icrc. org / Blood Bank: (713) 790-1200/ 211: United Way (Food stamps, United Way Help Line for Baby Supplies) / At Astrodome, a list, wall...PA system... people are calling out / Coast Guard #s (225) 925-7708; 7709; 3511 (get location, cell phone #, building address, on a roof..) / Medical volunteer? Go to Green Room, bottom floor of Astrodome. Bring your license...

Callers stumped me often. I could answer "How do I donate?" or "How do I come volunteer?" Everything else, well...the whiteboards never provided full answers. I tried to ask the supervisor. But that took too long, or, he didn't have real answers. If you worked in the phone bank, you needed to figure things out for yourself and fast.

Some things I said over my first six-hour shift:

"Right now, they're not giving out vouchers. I'm sorry. But you should go to a Red Cross shelter and register, so if they do give something, you're ready."

"I'm sorry it took you six hours to get through."

"You can try 'Somebody Cares.' It's an organization, I think. Maybe a church group. We're told they're giving out gas and grocery cards."

"You should try going to one of the smaller shelters. Just go there, and tell them that you'd like to take a couple, or a family with you, and they can help you. That's my advice to you, person to person. Go to a smaller church shelter, that way, you can feel out the situation, make sure you're comfortable, and they're

comfortable, you know?"

"If you know nurses, please tell them that yes, they need nurses. If there's anyone you can call and tell them, please let them know they need medical help."

"I'm sorry. You have to try to get through on those numbers. We don't have a list of the evacuees sheltering at the Astrodome."

"I'm sorry."

If I needed a break, I left the phone off the hook. A restaurant donated big aluminum pans of prepared food, but they were licked clean. The soda machine flashed empty, too. I asked a staff person if there was another machine. She said, "Upstairs." Then she turned to her colleague and asked, "Is she allowed up there?" The colleague laughed: "She can go get some soda."

The third floor felt hushed like an expensive department store in the morning. Yet I could still feel tension, expectancy. The pain of so many but I only heard one man in an office on his phone. I bought my water and got out.

In the meantime, I overheard that the Astrodome was taking walk-in volunteers. That's what I wanted. It was the whole reason I showed up here. But I didn't get up. I felt I should stick to the Red Cross phone banks. They'd get me over there when the time was right.

A new supervisor spoke up, an energetic woman who announced she'd only been there a day, but alas, she was picked. She helped us better than the man before. I took my seat and answered calls:

MOTHERS UNEARTHED

"If you want to be a Red Cross shelter, there is a meeting at 10 a.m. in Classrooms E & F."

"I know. I can't believe it either. I don't know how they can be abandoned like this."

"This is just me to you, OK? But you should try Lakewood Church, or Second Baptist Church. They're the more affluent churches here. I know they're helping people. This isn't the Red Cross talking, this is just me to you. I'm sorry that the Red Cross can't help you right now."

"I'm sorry, I'm just a volunteer."

"Sorry, you need to call the press officer."

"I'm sorry I can't be of better help. I know. I know. I'm sorry. Good luck."

"You know, you might try calling journalists. Call CNN. Try to get your story out there. I know it's not fair."

The man next to me answered a call a minute as well. We hadn't introduced ourselves. No time. Early 50s maybe. He looked like a vibrant upper-manager. We exchanged glances. Grimaced faces. Sighs.

A few hours later, he decided to get food. Fajitas. He came in from the suburbs to do this, he told me, and that's what he wanted. Did I want anything? No. He came back with white Styrofoam containers of chicken fajita nachos to share with our side of the room. He had to go. He brought them back just to feed us. I waved goodbye. I never learned his name.

I left my phone off the hook and ate.

On that Saturday, nearly a week after landfall, the American Red Cross had yet to offer financial assistance to Hurricane Katrina evacuees. No money. No grocery, no gasoline, no clothing vouchers. Not yet. Every second or third call, I choked up. Sometimes I cried. I tried hard to keep it together, because a crying phonebank woman helped no one. But someone talked about what they saw on TV. Someone told me their story of survival, and I told them that the Red Cross could do nothing for them.

A new batch of volunteers waited at the supervisor table. A Red Cross staffer appeared and asked us when we started working. If it was over four hours ago, it was time to leave. No exceptions. For me, it was over six hours and I was ready to keep going. But the staffer was firm. I went downstairs and signed up for another shift. The 3 a.m. shift, which was later that night.

Back home, I didn't sleep well. When I left at 2:40 a.m., I drove down empty freeways. I stopped at a 24-hour CVS to buy alcohol pads to wipe down the phones. I didn't want to get sick. This made me a little late.

When I showed up, they made me supervisor.

After I Sit Through a 2-hour Red Cross Orientation that Supposedly Qualifies Me to Volunteer Even though I've Supervised the Phonebank

I learned that the Red Cross didn't run the emergency shelters created in the Astrodome and Reliant Center stadiums nor the refuge created in the George R. Brown Convention Center. If you wanted to work there, you just had to show up.

Next day, I showed up.

At the Astrodome

My friend Ronnetta and I drove in together for a daytime shift and said we wanted to volunteer. They quickly took us in to work a lunch line. We handed out Chick-fil-A sandwiches. There were so many of us. Once Ronnetta and I finished our assigned tasks, we were somewhat jealous of other volunteers, not wanting to find ourselves "role-less." For now, the Houston volunteer response was incredible.

The shift went smoothly. No hitches.

Spreading the Word

Via email:

"Please. Go volunteer. You will not get jacked. These are normal people. Please help. And for those of you not down here, please hold charities accountable. All this money goes to them, but does it ever reach the survivors?"

Former Presidential Advisor Sidney Blumenthal wrote me back. He'd been a mentor to me for years. *Go listen to people*, he said. *Get stories down. Now.*

No, I thought. People still needed immediate aid. But at the Astrodome, and at the George R. Brown, there were so many volunteers. You could call it a glut. Each day I returned, there were more volunteers than the previous shift.

I listened to Sid.

* * *

Printiss Polk, *24, is a roofer, from the Ninth Ward of New Orleans. This interview was conducted on Sept. 5, 2005, one week after landfall and catastrophic flooding in New Orleans in the park across the street from the George R. Brown Convention Center in Houston, Texas. There were several people around, mostly men, sitting on the benches. The mood was calm. Towards the back of the park, several young men pass around cigarettes, some marijuana. On occasion, Printiss himself stood up to take a drag off a friend's cigarette. He appeared tired, as if still in a state of shock.*

Prime Coat

They flood us out. Every time water get high, only the downtown area goes through tragedies. It don't happen uptown. They sabotage us.

Down here, if you know these pumps don't work, you know it's hurricane season. Why we ain't got somebody down here? You got money to get somebody down here and fix the pipes.

When that hurricane was over and that rain stopped, that water was no higher than right here on my leg. Now all of sudden there's water over our house? At one time? I could see it if it's raining and the water rising — but the water just — you're just murdering people. That's straight up murder. You bring me to jail for shooting somebody in the head, and I'm going to bring you to jail for flooding these houses out.

These children. We people. You know, it's lives, man. Why you get in charge if you ain't going to do what you're really supposed to do? It was like they couldn't control the crime rate, drugs. It was at an all-time high. You know what I'm saying?

The hurricane was nothing but a prime coat for this real paint. Feel me? I think all this here was a cover-up to spread these people out. You know we can't really do nothing. We can't go against the grain.

I think people need to just open their eyes, really analyze life. I'm young, but I know more than the average person my age.

When the Hurricane Hit

When the hurricane hit, I was in the Florida Projects. In the Ninth Ward. Some people have first floors, but in our houses — they're new — they ain't like the old projects where they don't have no attics or nothing. They had attics. People would be able to get through their house to the top of their roof. That's what most of the people did when the water came so high. Across the Canal, if you weren't no good swimmer, or a young child or whatever, you died. And that's just — you know, that was that. A lot of people died, man.

The police was killing people. They was shooting people. I saw the police go really over the line. In our part of the city, in the Ninth Ward, I could understand — somebody started shooting at them in the helicopters, when they were rescuing people. I don't know who was shooting. I do know that the person that was shooting was shooting because all his family members had died in the house already. He couldn't get them out there. Too much water. The water was to the gutters of the roof. From right here the water — the water went from right here, to the gutter of the roof, in what, in a couple — in about 30 seconds? 40

seconds?

I was with my parents. Everybody got split up. Right now, I'm with a work partner of mine, his wife, and his kid, my godchild. I don't know where my sister at. My mama… my mama didn't leave. My mama stayed in the Palace Hotel. I don't even know — I didn't talk to her. I don't know when's the next time I'm going to talk to my mom. She don't have a cell phone or nothing.

Aftermath

I went all the way to the Fourth Ward to help my partner out with his family, my godchild. My children were in Pennsylvania at the time.

We had been through so many storms like this. Everybody was just worried about the storm. They didn't know that the water would ever be this high. You see what I'm saying? That the pipes were gonna bust, and then I actually walked down Claiborne and witnessed water coming up out the ground. Going into the water that was already there, like it was pumping from somewhere else. Y'all need to pump that into the river somewhere. These people too, just like you.

The water was high on Canal Street, six feet, seven feet. People dying. You walking past dead bodies. People stuck on poles. Poles going through — they had a man on Canal, right in the middle in the streetcar thing, with a pole stuck through his body. He was dead. Like he was drunk when the storm hit and fell dead on that pole. It went straight through him. Police just passing him. People's bodies, just…

One minute you see a baby crying with their mama, the wind blowing hard, the next minute you see a baby floating in water, dead. The wind was blowing at 160 miles per hour! How can a 7, 10 pound baby, a 2-week old baby, withstand all that wind? The mama's scared, she can't swim, because she ain't nothing but 14, 15. Some of the girls young in our projects, in the Florida Projects, with babies. Some of the girls — I don't know what's going on, but they start off at 13 and 14 years old with babies.

Older people dying. A lot of them dead.

The helicopters. The ha-ha-ha-ha-ha-ha [the blades], lights everywhere, boats, people panicking, screaming. Some people even diving and swimming in the water. It just was — it's like a lot of people just didn't have God in their life because something really drastic was about to happen to them. The spirit wasn't in them, so they couldn't, the spirit wasn't able to bear witness with the spirit, you see what I'm saying? And they was just asleep. They was awoke. But they was asleep? You feel me?

The water smelled like oil, gas, chemicals, stuff from the stores that people was breaking in. Dead bodies in the water. Dead dogs and cats, rats. Man, it took you to be strong just to walk through that water. The water was black. They had so much chemicals in that water, seem like if you would have lit a cigarette it would have blew up.

Helping People

I stayed in that water for like three days. Helping people and bringing people food and water.

First we built a raft. We went to an old tire shop, got some tires with air in them. Got some two-by-fours, three sheets of plywood, and built it.

We tried to save as many people as we could. They was in their houses, trying to stay in their houses. They didn't believe that the water was going to get higher. Everybody just had hope that the water was going to go down. The people didn't want to leave their homes.

What they would say? *Um, man I ain't leaving my home, what am I going to do? Where I'm going to — I'm going to have to start all over from scratch. I'm going to go somewhere and be a…*

Nobody wants to start all over. It's hard.

[Aside, to another young man] I told her all that, man. She know we built an ark. But she don't know about the five-month-old baby we carried through the storm. Through the water. He a little soldier, too. He a survivor. He five months old. It's raining. We walking through five and six feet of water with him. And he's holding us down. He's not crying or nothing. My partner was with his baby, Malik. My godchild.

We helped a lot of people. Me and Bobby, Printiss and Bobby. We did our thing, man. It got so bad, down in the Four, in the Fourth Ward, we had to take us a house that was up higher. And the people who was on the bridge by the Supderdome and had no water? We went to Kentwood [water company], opened up their thing, and took all the Kentwood trucks. We brought them on the bridge and gave everybody some water. We helped everybody. It was a storm. They couldn't do nothing with water and we needed it. We brought everybody who was out there gallons, big — they had big things that go in the machines. All them babies need that water. How they gonna drink a bottle without the water?

Dreaming a Sacred Garden

Vanessa Mártir

We moved into the first floor apartment on Palmetto Street in Bushwick, Brooklyn in the spring of 1980, the same year Reagan was elected. Sugar Hill Gang's Rapper's Delight brought a new music genre to the national stage, and a fierce heatwave hit NY, making August the hottest on record. I remember watching my mother standing by the window in the morning, surveying the backyard, coffee in hand, the steam fogging the glass. Piles of trash littered the yard, and the makeshift barriers that separated ours from the surrounding yards were made of plywood clumsily nailed together and falling apart, so there were gaping holes in spots. My eyes landed on the tree in the left corner of the yard.

Days later, mom climbed out the window and went to work. She swept up the years of garbage, bags that smelled of something dead or dying, cracked flower pots, a fork with twisted tongs; and threw it all over the dilapidated fence into the junk yard next door. This wasn't her littering. That yard was piled high with trash already. It was one of the many rubble strewn lots that dotted our neighborhood .

As mom toiled, I tiptoed past her and stood at the foot of the tree (I'd learn later that summer that it was a plum tree). A past resident had painted the trunk a dull salmon color. I picked at the chipping paint, pulling some trunk with it. I patted the tree and whispered, "Hi. I'm

Vanessa." I was a tiny four-year-old though I once overheard my mom tell someone: "Vanessa was always big. Even when she was little, she was big."

I started grappling up the trunk, scraping my legs and hands, peeling the pleather off my sneakers. At one point, a sharp branch stabbed into my side. I winced but kept climbing. Mom would scream at me to get down, "Te vas a dar un mal golpe, machua!" I wasn't bothered by being called a tomboy. I saw nothing wrong with doing things girls weren't "supposed to" do. Who made those rules anyway? Mom cut her eyes at me while I kept climbing. It took me weeks, but I didn't give up, and neither did mom.

My mother wasn't a Martha Stewart type of gardener with a sun hat and apron. She worked in a sofrito stained nightgown or t-shirt and shorts. She took to tilling the soil, using her right leg to push the old shovel into the ground to bring up the dark soil with squirming earthworms. When the earth wouldn't give, she got on all fours and used her hands. Then she went out and bought the seeds. Each packet had a picture of the potential inside: peppers, tomatoes, eggplant, squash, herbs like peppermint, cilantro and rosemary, flowers like geraniums and sunflowers. She handled the seeds with a tenderness I envied.

By mid-summer, we had a lush garden, and I'd learned how to climb the plum tree. The sunflowers grew so tall and heavy, mom tied them to the fence using an old shoelace. We ate from the bounty of that yard every day—sofrito made with peppers, cilantro and recao, diced tomato and cucumber salad. It was from my perch on a branch that I watched my mom's joy when she first saw evidence of baby tomatoes and eggplants.

MOTHERS UNEARTHED

I was in my forties and a mother myself when mom revealed how she learned to garden. Up until then, her stories of her childhood in Honduras were of hunger and suffering. We were poor, but I didn't know the hunger mom spoke of.

Her face grew wistful and nostalgic, the way it does when she speaks of her great-grandmother Tinita, who mom says "fue mi madre." They lived in the campo outside of the city of La Ceiba, where Tinita taught my mother to toil the earth, planting vegetables, flowers and herbs. They grew enough to eat and sell, and lived comfortably, though not lavish. Mom laughed when she spoke of the stubborn mule they owned. Whenever the mule was tired, it sat and refused to move no matter how Tinita slapped his rear. Once, he sat in the middle of the river as they were crossing. Tinita had to unload the goods he was carrying, and they sat at the river's edge for hours until the donkey decided to move again. Mom's eyes welled and she blinked hard a few times. "Ahí siempre tuvimos de comer." In the city the land was scarce, so they couldn't plant enough to feed themselves. "Ahí sufrimos," mom said. When I asked why they moved to the city, mom shrugged. That's where the work was.

The next summer, I started climbing into the junkyard next door when mom wasn't looking. Piled high with old tires, license plates with sharp, curled edges, lumber with rusted nails jutting out, an occasional needle, cables, wires, rats, feral cats, rubble. Shrubs and trees pushed up through all that trash, and at the height of the summer, the foliage grew so thick that if you looked at the right angle, you could almost forget where you were. It was a jungle to my five, six, seven-year-old eyes. The mounds were ancient structures built into the ground.

Somehow the dark magic within had been unleashed, and I was called there, the female Indiana Jones, to save the world from its wrath. It was in that garden and that junkyard that I became fascinated with the earth's fauna and flora; all things green and squirmy.

* * *

My mother was still gardening when I left at 13 to attend boarding school hundreds of miles away. She stopped when she grew tired of the neighbors littering her garden with their trash. She brought her plants into her tiny, railroad style apartment where they now crowd every room.

I don't have pictures of my mother's garden, but I have images of the neighborhood that surrounded it. I remember seeing the news of Beirut after the bombings in the early 80s and thinking it looked like home.

Between 1965 and 1980, there were over a million fires in NYC. Referred to as the Fire Wars, the South Bronx is most notorious for the aftermath, but Bushwick was just as devastated. Occurring during the city's worst fiscal crisis, when fire houses were being shuttered and the culmination of redlining, mortgage scams and insurance fraud left black and brown neighborhoods in shambles. Then the blackout happened in July of 1977.

Neil deMause writes of the Brooklyn Wars: "It instantly became part of the legend of 1970s New York: the night that the final indignity was visited upon the dead-broke, arson-wracked city. And no part of the five boroughs was to become more associated with the blackout than the old north Brooklyn neighborhood of Bushwick. When the lights went out, hundreds of people began breaking into stores along Broadway, the southern boundary separating Bushwick from Bedford-Stuyvesant, pulling down security gates, smashing windows, hauling off furniture, TVs, whatever they could carry. On the commercial strip beneath the elevated J train tracks, 45 stores were set ablaze; a few days later, what became known as the "All Hands Fire" started in an abandoned factory, taking out 23 more buildings in the heart of the neighborhood."[1]

Bushwick was left a neighborhood dotted with abandoned and burnt out buildings, and trash and rubble strewn lots.

My mother built a garden oasis in that war zone. I've carried it with me since.

* * *

When I became a mother, I shared my love and respect for nature with my daughter, taking her to parks around the city and hiking their trails. Not Central Park so much because it's planted, and Seneca Village, home to the largest number of African-American property owners in NY before the Civil War, was razed to create it. We'd take hours-long train rides to the beaches, Rockaway, Brighton, Coney Island. This was how I introduced her to the idea of a creator/higher power when she was in Pre-K; if I believe in anything, I believe in nature. "God is in everything, mamita. In the trees, the clouds, the birds. God is in you." She started interrogating this on our commutes to school. She'd point at a flower, a lamp post, a traffic light and ask: "Is God in that flower? Is God in that lamp? Is God in that light?" Once, a man walked by with his dog. When the dog stopped to do its business, my daughter giggled

---

1   deMause, Neil. "How The 1977 Blackout Was Bushwick's Grimmest Moment." Gothamist, 28 Sept. 2016, gothamist.com/news/how-the-1977-blackout-was-bushwicks-grimmest-moment.

and looked up at me, her supernova smile taking over her entire face. "Mommy, is God in poop?" I laughed too. "Sure, God is in poop, too."

* * *

Wherever I've traveled or moved to, I've searched out woods. The redwood forests of Berkeley and Oakland. A tree lined trail in Decatur, Georgia. The deep woods of Portland, Oregon.

At home in NYC, it was the old-growth forest of Inwood Hill Park that saved me when my brother Juan Carlos died in 2013. I walked paths created centuries ago by the Lenape, some so steep you have to grapple up. I discovered their ancient healing circles that are now being maintained by Tainos.

I went into the forest one day, a mantra in my head: "I need you to hold me. I need you to hold me."

My face was streaked with tears, snot dripped out of my nose.

It started in front of me, blue jays chirping so loud, I stopped. Sparrows to my right. Red cardinals to my left. Titmice and nuthatches behind me. The birds carried my broken heart into their throats.

I was being held in bird song.

* * *

Once, when mom had been gardening in that yard for years, she sent me out to gather tomatoes and peppers. "I need them for the sofrito," she said. Small piles of onions and garlic lay on the cutting board on top of the table. The day before I'd noticed that the tomatoes were red and green. I turned them over like I'd seen her do. They were firm to the touch.

I gasped at the scene that greeted me. The rats from the junkyard next door had feasted on mom's vegetables. Peppers, tomatoes and eggplant lay scattered about, bitten into in chunks. I could make out their teeth marks on the flesh. A few hung limply on the bush. The rats had even bitten the flower heads off their stems. I gathered what I could and climbed back into the apartment.

"Mommy," I said in almost a whisper. "The rats ate them. These are the only ones left."

Mom slammed down the knife she was using to chop the cilantro and stomped out to the yard. She cursed and yanked up some of the bushes. I ran to hide in the room I shared with my sister and brother, and didn't come out until she called us for dinner.

Mom eventually brought her plants inside. "Here I can protect them." That backyard is back to the condition it was when we first moved in. She still has plants all over her small, railroad style apartment, the same one she raised us in in Bushwick, perched at the top of cabinets and bookshelves, on window gates, hanging from hooks in the ceiling, on the table in her living room, a table that is made for four but can only seat one due to all those plants.

Her light bill is always astronomically high, nearly $300 a month, because of the lights she keeps on 24/7 for her plants. "They're my babies now," she says.

* * *

It was the deck overlooking the park that sold the Bronx apartment to me in late 2016 when my now-wife and I moved in together. For years, I dreamed of living somewhere that looked out onto a forest. I'd imagined plants hanging on windows, and a backyard garden like the one my mother had. I hadn't inherited my mother's green thumb, so I didn't know how I'd care for all that greenery. The only plant I hadn't killed was a Golden Pothos, also known as Devil's Ivy because it's nearly indestructible. I named her "La Doña," and gave friends cuttings when they visited.

When you fantasize of another life, you can dream up anything, until you get the chance and you do. Over the years, I expanded my vision and my construction worker wife helped bring it to reality. She hung lights, put up hooks, installed shelves and planters.

When the pandemic hit, I set my eyes to the deck. If we couldn't go anywhere, I would create a space where we could relax and remember hope, despite the multiple ongoing horrors happening in the world—COVID-19, unarmed black and brown folks being murdered by police, the injustices happening at the border, climate change ravaging the earth as evidenced by extreme weather, like Hurricane Harvey, heat waves that killed people and livestock, droughts that caused famine, flooding that swept people's homes and lives away.

I recruited my family and we started germinating seeds, and I started buying plants and flowers from the many vendors that sprouted up around the hood.

At first the nonstop blare of ambulance and police sirens was startling, but they eventually became white noise, like the ubiquitous fire truck sirens of my childhood.

We joined the many New Yorkers who at 7pm, headed to their windows and balconies to applaud the frontline workers fighting the pandemic. There was something at once heartbreaking and hopeful about the chorus of clapping, cheering, pots and drums beating, cowbells clanking, a saxophone a few times, played to the tune of Sinatra's "New York, New York."

It didn't take long for me to see that I did on my deck what my mother did in our backyard in the 80s: I created a garden oasis in a warzone.

* * *

Throughout the six years my wife and I have been together, we've escaped numerous times to the woods of upstate NY, NJ and PA. We met in the woods of Hart, Michigan, so our love for nature was something we bonded over immediately.

We talked about the dream we shared of living in the country, but it seemed like an impossible dream— I was a single mom and a struggling artist; she'd never met someone she wanted to do that with. It was on that deck that we started envisioning a garden on a land that was ours.

In August of 2020, we rented a house in Phoenicia, NY, to get away and celebrate my daughter's 16th birthday. A stream ran through the back of the house, there were hiking trails steps away, and we couldn't see or hear the neighbors, something unheard of by apartment dwellers like us. It was a blissful five days. When we returned, we were ready.

By mid-summer my deck garden was so lush, there was barely room for anyone but my plant babies.

This is what joy looks like.

When we came to see the house in Orange County in upstate NY in October of 2020, we walked the 6.5 acres of land for 45 minutes before even stepping into the house. A fenced-in area had once been a garden. There were gaping holes in the fencing, and it was laden with fallen branches and a huge mound of ash and charcoal from the wood burning stove, but I saw the potential immediately. I thought of my mother's garden. When we went into the house, I knew the room that looked out onto the garden would be my writing room. Suddenly we understood what our realtor, a sassy Dominicana, meant when she said: "You'll know your house when you see it."

* * *

We moved in in February, after delaying the move twice due to blizzard conditions. It snowed 28 inches, and then inches more over a matter of days. Neighbors who lived in the area for over forty years said they'd never experienced a winter like this.

I decided quickly that I was going to follow indigenous agricultural practices which hold that you can't, shouldn't plant on land you're new to for an entire growing season. I was there to be a steward. To let the land teach me. To learn from its gifts.

The lessons and signs were (still are) everywhere. When my brother died in 2013, I bought my mom and I bleeding heart tinctures. They help with grief.

I discovered peony bushes on the side of the house and along the circular driveway. Peonies were my bridal flower.

We have several hydrangea and hibiscus bushes on the land. These were

Bleeding hearts were one of the first flowers to bloom on our land.

my great grandmother Tinita's favorite flowers.

I've dreamed of sharing this land with my daughter and her children, if she has any, and the family she builds. This spring, I spent days clearing out the 25 x 30 foot garden while my wife repaired the holes in the fencing and added vinyl panels. There's an old, sacred energy about the space. I can feel the care that was put in the details, like the stones that line the perimeter to keep out burrowing animals like rabbits; a hydrangea bush marks due north and the entrance to the garden is due south.

As I tilled the land, I imagined sending my daughter out to get me ingredients for sofrito—onions, scallions, ajicitos, garlic, cilantro, recao, a bit of celery if my taste buds ask for it.

I imagine her cutting a fat tomato, like my sister did when we were kids, sprinkling some salt on it and taking a big bite, the juice dripping down her chin. Her eyes closed in utter delight and ecstasy.

I imagine sharing this bounty with my family. Making boxes of vegetation for my mom, titi, and grandma, and my sister-friends and chosen family as well. A CSA of sorts.

I dream this while worrying that extreme weather fueled by climate change will make this dream impossible.

* * *

I lived in NYC in 2012 when Hurricane Sandy hit. The storm created a record 32-foot tall wave in NY Harbor, and was the strongest storm to make landfall in the Northeast.

In an article titled "The only storm that scared me," meteorologist John Davitt wrote: "The storm was straight out of worst-case storm scenarios that researchers modeled over the past 20 years when doing studies on possible hurricane impacts for New York City."[2]

Over the course of 48 hours, wind, rain, and water destroyed more than 300 homes and left hundreds of thousands without power.

Millions of gallons of seawater flooded the subways. A crane was ripped off a building by the winds. The storm left many New Yorkers vulnerable with limited access to food, drinking water, healthcare and other critical services. Numerous hospitals were closed and evacuated. I remember the aftermath: the fallen trees in Inwood Hill Park, how impossible it was to get gas for days on end.

My beloved city that never sleeps was paralyzed. There's evidence[3] that climate change very likely made Sandy's impacts worse than they otherwise would have been.

I thought of Hurricane Sandy when Ida hit in August of 2021. The rain pelting the roof and windows sounded like small fists, pummeling. I watched from the deck doors.

The wind reminded me of the Fulton Street stop on the A/C line, specifically the sound the train makes when it's resurfacing from the

---

2   Davitt, M. J. (2020, October 28). Remembering Hurricane Sandy: The Only Storm That Ever Scared Me. Spectrum News NY1. https://www.ny1.com/nyc/all-boroughs/weather/2020/10/28/the-only-storm-that-ever-scared-me--a-meteorologist-remembers-hurricane-sandy

3   Freedman, Andrew. (2012, November 1). How Global Warming Made Hurricane Sandy Worse. Climate Central. https://www.climatecentral.org/news/how-global-warming-made-hurricane-sandy-worse-15190

tunnel under the East River that leads to Brooklyn. You hear it before you see the lights of the train—a low roar that builds to a whooshing and rumbling when the wind rushes in, blowing your hair everywhere and pushing your body a few inches.

The trees bent and swayed at impossible angles. The rain fell in sheets. I wondered when it would stop or at least slow down. It didn't. For hours.

The storm killed at least 49 people across the tri-state area, sparked massive flooding, and left hundreds of thousands of people without power.

My family and I were lucky. We never lost power though it flickered a few times. There was some flooding on the ground floor and our roof leaked a bit, but all in all, we were fortunate. An acquaintance had three feet of water in her basement, and discovered that her insurance, like most homeowner's insurance, didn't cover the flood damage.

Tripti Bhattacharya, an assistant professor of earth and environmental sciences at Syracuse University told NPR: "A storm like this would have been exceptionally rare 20 or 50 years ago. But we have to start thinking about it becoming the norm as the climate warms."[4]

I've heard that severe weather like this will become more commonplace. NBC News reported just the other day: "A child born in 2021 will live on average through seven times as many heat waves, twice as many

---

4   Chappell, Bill. "Why Ida Hit The Northeast So Hard, 1,000 Miles Away From Its Landfall." NPR, 13 Sept. 2021, www.npr.org/2021/09/03/1034058911/hurricane-ida-climate-change-northeast-flooding-rainfall.

wildfires and nearly three times as many droughts, crop failures and river floods as their grandparents, according to a study released Sunday that looks at how different generations will be affected by climate change."[5]

When it will be our turn? We live at the foot of a mountain, surrounded by swampland, bogs and ponds. Will this always be here or will climate change and severe weather take this dream from us? This dream that started in my mother's garden in Bushwick.

People's houses are being swept away by overflowing rivers, land and rock slides. Wildfires on the west coast have caused some gorgeous sunsets in these parts, but there's nothing beautiful about the reasons why it's happening.[6]

Will I get a chance to become indigenous to this land? Indigenous defined the way Potowatomi writer and scientist Robin Wall Kimmerer explains it in her opus *Braiding Sweetgrass: Indigenous Wisdom, Scientific Knowledge, and the Teachings of Plants*: "For all of us, becoming indigenous to a place means living as if your children's future mattered, to take care of the land as if our lives, both material and spiritual depended on it."

Insects are vanishing at alarming rates.[7] Will my grandchildren never

5   Chow, Denise, et al. "U.N. Releases Blistering Assessment on the State of Climate Change." NBC News, 9 Aug. 2021, www.nbcnews.com/science/environment/un-releases-blistering-assessment-state-climate-change-rcna1622.

6   Borunda, Alejandra. "The Science Connecting Wildfires to Climate Change." National Geographic, 3 May 2021, www.nationalgeographic.com/science/article/climate-change-increases-risk-fires-western-us.

7   "Insects Are Vanishing from Our Planet at an Alarming Rate. But There

know what it's like to feel a katydid latch onto their finger, like dozens of tiny, sticky graspers?

Will they never get to marvel and laugh at the noisy frog orgy that commences on the pond on the first day of spring?

Will they get to hear the screams and barks of the foxes during mating

---

Are Ways to Help Them." The Guardian, 29 Oct. 2021, www.theguardian.com/commentisfree/2021/sep/21/insects-vanishing-alarming-help.

season?

Will they get that sense of awe when they hear the screech of a barn owl, the hoot of a great horned owl through the canopy?

I worked so hard for this life on this land.

I am doing my part. I've become aware of how much trash we produce and am working on changing that. I save the paper to burn in the wood burning stove. This city girl has started several composting piles on our land. I spent the winter saving and grounding the shells of eggs we've eaten, and stored them for use in our garden.

I can do so much, but the world's biggest emitters of greenhouse gasses are corporations who, despite knowing the damage they're doing to the environment, continue with no regard for the future of our planet. There are so many plans and hopes I have for this land, for me, my family, blood and chosen, and future generations of our lineage. Will climate change fueled by human greed and hubris take that away?

I am overwhelmed by climate change and global warming. But inaction never affects change. I can do my part on these few acres.

I think of Agent Smith's words in The Matrix: "Every mammal on this planet instinctively develops a natural equilibrium with the surrounding environment but you humans do not. You move to an area and you multiply and multiply until every natural resource is consumed and the only way you can survive is to spread to another area. There is another organism on this planet that follows the same pattern. Do you know what it is? A virus."

This doesn't have to be true. We don't have to exist like viruses. This hasn't always been the way.

Who can we look to in order to learn how to live in harmony with the earth? What adjustments can we make? Are we willing?

For the benefit of the earth and future generations? I read[8] that since wolves were reintroduced back into Yellowstone in the 90s, an unexpected trophic cascade of ecological change occurred, including helping beaver populations flourish and bringing back aspen and other vegetation. Some[9] even claim that the wolves changed the rivers by feasting on elk that overgrazed. The vegetation was able to grow, thus reducing erosion and stabilizing riverbanks, so the rivers meandered less, the channels deepened and small pools formed.

How can we re-establish this natural equilibrium with the earth, the way the wolves have in Yellowstone?

Kimmerer writes: "How in our modern world, can we find one way to understand the earth as a gift again, to make our relationship with the world sacred again?...even in market economy, can we behave 'as if' the living world were a gift?"

I see my mother's hands in the dirt. I smell the mossy, wet of freshly

---

8   GrrlScientist. "How Wolves Change Rivers - Video." The Guardian, 14 Feb. 2018, www.theguardian.com/science/grrlscientist/2014/mar/03/how-wolves-change-rivers.

9   Farquahr, Brodie. "Wolf Reintroduction Changes Ecosystem in Yellowstone." Yellowstone National Park, 1 July 2021, www.yellowstonepark.com/things-to-do/wildlife/wolf-reintroduction-changes-ecosystem.

upturned soil. I see my hands, the soil caked under my nails and in the creases of my skin. I am demonstrating to my daughter the nourishment the earth can gift you if you take care of it.

I started collecting wildflowers last spring. I only ever take enough to make a few bouquets. The intention is to brighten our home; to see my daughter smile when she notices the one by her bed and my wife's eyes twinkle when I place one on the table when we sit for dinner; to feel that deep exhale my body releases when I'm writing or teaching and look over to see the sunlight shining on the bouquet.

Photographs by and courtesy of the author, unless otherwise noted.

For more images from the garden and beyond, please view this piece in the digital journal via the QR code or asterixjournal.com

Basil

January Gill O'Neil

On those afternoons
when I feel most fraught,
broke as a joke,
I breathe with the trees.

Yes, my children's laughter.
Yes, my dog's wagging tail.
Yes, when my lover puts his lips on me
wherever he wants.

There are places where sweet tea
with lemon is served year-round.
Think of it! Fresh brewed.
Frosted glass.

Because some days there is no mercy,
I'm counting my remaining supply
of moments in the troubled light.
When I tear basil from the garden

I nurtured all summer,
even as it begins to bolt,

MOTHERS UNEARTHED

the smell lingers on my fingers
long after I crush it.

Spaceship

Emily Barton

The unmasked lead their gaggles of unmasked children into Target. They walk out pushing red plastic trolleys loaded with plastic bags full of food to sustain their bodies, clothing to cover their bodies, soaps to clean their bodies and homes, toys and gadgets to entertain the children. The goods go into the hatchbacks of their white Escalades, their white GMCs, all the vehicles swollen, white, gas-guzzling. The plastics are destined for the trash or Lake Erie.

My children stay home. I wear a mask as I push my trolley around the store. The unmasked glance at me, perhaps afraid I'm unvaccinated, or sure they know my political affiliation from the fact I'm wearing the mask. They'd be correct. I believe they're not wearing masks because of what they'd called freedom, though you might more correctly define it as liberty or license. Freedom to do what you want. Freedom to do what you want even if it puts others' lives at risk.

* * *

I work as a college professor, so I spend hours at a time talking in classrooms with students, and work closely with colleagues in our offices and at seminar tables. Faculty at many institutions feel concerned about in-person teaching because of the risk of infection. As the fall semester begins in September 2021, our institution mandates vaccination for all students, faculty, and staff, though there are no stated consequences for noncompliance. Students and faculty mask in the classroom; faculty and staff are to mask except when alone in our offices. To me these measures feel relatively safe, although one of my children isn't yet old enough to be vaccinated, so remains at higher risk. In my office cluster there are also three other parents of children too young for vaccination, one mother herself immune-compromised, and a woman who cares for her frail elderly parents. Several academic programs share the office suite, and people from several more come through to use our copy machine and wash mugs in our sink.

A coworker who refuses to get vaccinated sits at a centrally located desk. She eats vegan, she says, and gets sunshine and exercise every day, so her immune system is strong; and God will choose who lives and who dies. She sits at her desk, does a good job, and is in all other respects a kind and thoughtful coworker, though she endangers the elderly parents, the four unvaccinated children, and the colleague down the hall who recently finished cancer treatment.

Meanwhile, the ongoing brute work of converting the campus's massive antiquated heating system to geothermal continues. Shade trees down, trenches dug, temporary pedestrian bridges, detours, looming piles of infrastructural equipment, all of it looking like 1960s sci-fi. The campus expects to be carbon neutral by 2025. Such a huge, optimistic investment in a future I hope we all live to see.

* * *

My whole childhood I believed I had less than other people. I did have less than the girls at my school, with their semi-circular driveways and baby grands and horses, the high-mounded mulch around their trees. Yet in college, I learned that my family had more wealth than 96% of the families on earth. I was rich not with riding lessons but with reliable shelter, sufficient food, clean water, access to toilets. This stark, basic fact about the world had escaped me because I was a teenager, and no doubt also because of relative privilege. The parts of the world in which you had to walk a mile to use a toilet were too far for me to see. I felt chastened.

* * *

A short list of national events that have filled me with rage:

The assertion that Al Gore, the more qualified presidential candidate, would have fared better had he been more likable.

Hanging chads.

Our current inaction on the climate crisis, which follows in a direct line from those hanging chads.

Mitch McConnell blocking Merrick Garland's appointment to the Supreme Court, then subsequently turning tail when his argument would apply to Amy Coney Barrett.

Walking around singing Lin-Manuel Miranda's "Never Gonna Be President Now" when the pee-pee tape news broke, then watching that horrible predictometer on the *New York Times* website while people elected him President.

Who we had as President when COVID hit.

MOTHERS UNEARTHED

His selecting three Supreme Court Justices.

Dobbs vs. Jackson.

West Virginia vs. EPA.

Big oil, and how deeply it's enmeshed with money and power.

On a smaller scale:

Being the last person admitted to my grad-school class, the only one not awarded a fellowship; being told this, it seemed, to keep me in my place.

Men looking at my breasts while conversing with me.

The implied threat when men on the street order me to smile.

An older colleague putting his hand on my leg under the dinner table. Having to ask an older woman colleague if she could make him stop, because I believed I'd be the one to suffer at that institution if, as a visitor, I filed a complaint against tenured faculty. Whatever she told him worked.

At a different institution, my department chair: "Well, don't you look *cute*."

When he had scheduled an all-faculty meeting during Kol Nidre, I told him I found this religiously insensitive. He replied, "I think I've been very sensitive. I scheduled it early enough that you should be able to get to your *little dinner thing*."

* * *

The base state of motherhood is rage. Rage at the baby itself. Babies sucking and grabbing at and licking and biting my nipples all day and night, a sensation that makes me recoil and that now I could never escape, even in sleep. Then lack of sleep. Not for days, weeks, or months, but years—years still ongoing, even with my younger son in third grade. Years since I've slept through a night.

The breast pump. More sucking. Cleaning and storing, scrounging out time and space to use it from already-full days. Sharing my office with another person, who fortunately is kind and has raised three babies of her own. We still have to negotiate it. Rage at the way our culture devalues motherhood. How expensive daycare is. How easy it would be to quit my job and not pay for daycare, if only I didn't want to work, if only I wanted to spend my time with babies. How much pressure there is to do Mommy-and-Me classes, and how, when I go, I have little in common with the other women beyond that all of us have babies. How you can't send a child to daycare if he's under the weather. Someone has to lose a day of work. How, if you're nursing, it really has to be you. How once you are done nursing, your husband, being a man, has no workplace protections on the basis of parental status, so his boss threatens to fire him if he misses days caring for a sick child. Thenceforward, until years later when he gets a better job, my work and my time are more often compromised. My job and also my writing.

The school calls the mother first if it's closing or the child has fallen ill and needs to be picked up or has a bloody nose or has wet his pants and needs someone to bring dry pants. The school assumes you're at home, perhaps watching TV, or that if you have a job, it's a secondary job, an extra job, because your husband has the real job. There's no consideration for women who want to work, or have to work, who have the main jobs themselves, or for lesbian or non-binary parents or single moms, or families with no moms at all.

Rage, all the time. Ongoing incoherent rage at the child because you did not know when people said parenting was a tough job that *this* was what they meant, and more significantly rage because the whole system is stacked against you if you choose to work, which I do, and also choose to have children, which I did, and would do again. I would do it again. I love their questions, talents, and sense of humor. I'm grateful to be able to help them grow into thoughtful, resilient adults. They're good people, interesting and fun. But I will be punished for wanting and having both. I will continue to feel my blood pressure in my throat each time I encounter the punishment.

* * *

The slow-building boredom-rage of spending a whole day following a toddler's whims, walking down the street at the rate of one block an hour as he stops to examine each pebble, each leaf; making the lunch he requests and having him fling it across the room because it isn't the lunch he thought he wanted. The slow-building boredom-rage of listening to a child talk about Pokémon, or of reading a Pokémon manual to him aloud, or of reading the first chapter of a third-rate book to him for the umpteenth time when he keeps falling asleep before you get farther. The book is terrible, but cannot be as terrible as rehearsing its first chapter again and again.

* * *

Other people's judgment, if you love your work, if you would rather do it than spend all your time with your children; your rage against them. Your rage about other people's concerns about your child's gender presentation. Why his hair is long, why he prefers bright colors, why he wants to carry a small tote with his rocks and plastic animals in it, why his clothes don't proclaim allegiance to corporate sports empires. Why you cloth-diaper when disposables are readily available. Why you still carry him in a baby carrier: "He'll never learn to walk," though the person with the opinion might very well be pushing, or have pushed, their own baby in a stroller. Stroller babies learn to walk fine, but carried babies are spoiled.

Each time this comes up—it happens day after day, week after week, year after year—I answer, I don't think our ancestors had strollers when they crossed the land bridge from Asia, or when the Sea of Reeds parted and they escaped from Mitzrayim. They did carry babies in slings, though. This argument elicits puzzled stares, either about the invention of strollers, paleoanthropology, or Judaism, or about why I'd scoff at prevailing wisdom, shared only to help me. Stroller plastic will persist unchanged for a thousand years in landfills along with disposable diapers. Cloth diapers and baby wraps biodegrade. But people shrug. It's a free country, the shrugs might say, though that has only ever been true for certain people. Rage against how so many in your society view your choices and the way you parent. One day, as I walk with Baby #2 in a wrap on my back, a black woman pulls her car over. "That's the way to do it, mama," she shouts. "That's how we do it back home in Kenya! Good for you!" My eyes instantly sting with tears. I thank her, wave, want to prolong the encounter, but she pulls back into traffic on the busy street.

MOTHERS UNEARTHED

* * *

Where I grew up—Westfield, New Jersey—felt safe from the world's disasters: earthquakes, tornados, tsunamis. I visited California for the first time as a teen, and felt an earthquake while sleeping one night. It wasn't huge, magnitude five. Still, it scared me, made me wonder how anyone could choose to settle atop that kind of instability. Now most of the world is unstable. Towns like mine flood. People paddle down streets in canoes. They drown in their bloated cars. It happens to New Orleans, it happens to Mumbai, but when it happens to New Jersey, or to quaint hamlets in Germany—

* * *

Even if you start out healthy, middle class, white, with access to medical care in the developed world, pregnancy is fraught with peril. Pregnancy books describe all possible disasters, as if this is what they want you to do, worry about what can go wrong. If you start having babies in your late thirties, as I did, there is a whole lot of doom talk about "geriatric pregnancy" and "advanced maternal age." You could have had children while in your reproductive prime if you hadn't been so focused on your career. As with all things related to motherhood, it's your fault.

My first pregnancy devolved into preeclampsia and six weeks of bed rest. Then an emergency C-section after a failed external version, an attempt to turn a breech baby. The ultrasound showed oligohydramnios—a precipitous loss of amniotic fluid—and the baby went into cardiac distress. For the duration of my second pregnancy, I had hyperemesis gravidarum, uncontrolled vomiting. Not morning sickness: This is vomiting day and night for the whole pregnancy, not being able to keep down a teaspoon of water; needing to go to the hospital to be rehydrated and pumped full of drugs, then vomiting again within an hour of getting home. I still went to work. On the day I gave birth to my second child, I was so malnourished I weighed 118 pounds, counting him still in there. That birth was traumatic too. I was permitted to V-BAC (have a vaginal birth after delivery), as many people are not because hospitals fear uterine rupture and lawsuits, but he got stuck and had to be suctioned out, via a botched episiotomy that took months and then years to heal.

These were good births with fortunate outcomes. After all that—a baby. At once so fragile and so fierce in its determination to live.

After birth, your energy diverts to mere survival, yours and the baby's. You nurse the baby day and night. You nurse the baby through gas and hiccups and fevers and hand, foot, and mouth disease (not hoof, I still have to tell myself, not hoof-and-mouth) and impetigo and projectile vomiting and explosive diarrhea, through learning to sit, crawl, walk, run, ride a scooter, ride a bike, climb, pet friendly dogs and avoid vicious ones, put 100,000 variously toxic and choke-on-able objects in his mouth. You take him to the doctor when he's ill, to urgent care when he's injured, to the ER when he's injured and the urgent care is closed. Hours arguing with health insurance because this is America, where we pay the world's highest rates for substandard care and then have to pay more thanks to for-profit insurers' and hospitals' inept billing.

And there is no value to this work, not to anyone else. There's no break at work or in the schedule at which writers are supposed to produce books, very little sympathy from anyone around you unless they too are living through this period. A friend's mother says, "No one cares about you after the baby comes out." No one cares about you after the baby comes out. You work to keep a roof over your heads and because you love to work, love *your* work. You bathe and feed and dress, you mend clothes, you buy clothes, you sort through hand-me-downs, you play stacking games and recite the alphabet and sing "I've Been Working on the Railroad" and "Good Night, Irene" until you wish *you* could jump in the river and drown, you read to at night, while doing all the work of your work. You make sure your children focus on their schoolwork. You help them when they're struggling, you practice math with them in the car, you make sure they get enough sleep and drink water and eat a variety of foods, you give them a Jewish education at home (Shabbat, holidays, practicing Jewish values) and in synagogue and Hebrew school, you prepare them for college and for adult life (take these steps to address an empty toilet paper roll; this is how you fold and sort laundry; here's why a pawn shop is less awesome than it sounds; be polite to older people), you hope they can get scholarships because your two full-time jobs can't keep you all housed and fed and support two college tuitions. You do all of this. You keep them safe in all these ways. You've always known you can't protect them from accidents, fatal illnesses. You know the polar ice caps are melting and coral reefs are dying and there's a monstrous floating island of plastic trash in the Pacific. But the past eighteen months, you never imagined. All of these horrors have something in common, though, which is that countless people are at fault, while countless others have to pay the price.

* * *

May 2022: I dream about giving birth to a third child. The Labor & Delivery ward triages women in kennels. Each cage holds a laboring woman, sometimes along with a partner or a medical practitioner, sometimes with machines. I refuse to go into my kennel, and instead walk free in the corridors between them, screaming, leaking blood and fluids. At one point I vomit on the ward's scale, and in the dream have the idea that I am making performance art.

* * *

In March 2020, the day the college announces its closure also happens to be Purim. I am wearing a Gryffindor uniform, including sweater and repp tie, when the Dean calls an emergency all-faculty meeting. That morning, it felt fun to Hermione myself, tie the tie. At the meeting, I feel embarrassed to be the only one in a costume, the person who didn't understand the somberness of the day.

Public schools close outright, and you and your partner keep working full-time—teaching online, from home—while the children bounce off the walls of your small house. Your employer recognizes that during this time parents and other caretakers (like my colleague who cares for her parents) shoulder a huge burden, but takes no meaningful steps to lighten that load. It would be impossible, the institution states, for parents to receive a course reduction or temporarily to reduce office hours or committee responsibilities—parents can't receive money to offset the cost of babysitting should babysitting ever again become possible—despite that these ordinary job responsibilities have become actually impossible if you have school-age-or-littler kids at home, who are now your responsibility every hour of every day and night, while the lives of the childless and those with grown children have in many cases increased in terms of stress and dread, but that's all.

Until May 2020, the kids are loose in your house, tuning in for an hour a day of Zoom school, and otherwise bored and wild from so much unstructured time, while you and your husband have your computers at home and continue to teach your freaked out, dislocated students virtually. The children, like much of society, no longer want to get dressed, and now continuously wear pajamas. No one knows whether it's safe for kids from different families to play together, so they don't; they call wistfully over the fence to the kids next door. Your next-door neighbor, one parent of those children, is a brilliant artist with whom you typically converse about art-making, academia, and the news as well as about your children, but now you both feel your brains have atrophied. You leave perfume samples in each other's mailboxes and then text about them—a small, sensory connection in an otherwise now completely disembodied world.

In June, the Center for Disease Control determines that outdoor playdates of kids whose families are in a pod together are low risk, so you pod up with the family next door. Now the kids can play, and you sometimes have an adult conversation outside. Then ensues a long summer of no camp and no babysitting. You can't write, or plan your fall courses, because you entertain children all day. You can't think a thought through to completion, because exactly like when they were babies and toddlers, they are interrupting you, asking for things, yanking on you, in your physical space all the time. Dust accrues, dishes, garbage, toilet smells. You can't see your seventy-nine-year-old father because he's too far away to pod with, too far away to drive to in a single day, and you don't want to risk giving him the illness by stopping at a hotel or a restaurant, stopping for gas.

When the kids go back to school in September 2020, it's online. The best part: seventh-grader, in band each morning at 8:10, blowing his trombone in his office, which was formerly your office. He's good at the trombone, the sound is crisp and clear, if extremely loud. If you walk the dog early in the morning, you can hear it a block away, with the windows closed. Neighbors claim it doesn't bother them. Worst parts: seventh- and second-graders, bored out of their minds all day, finagling ways to play bootleg versions of Minecraft on their school computers and asking for snack after snack after snack. Ten snacks a day, fifteen. Increasing pickiness about snacks; diminishing willingness to accept fruits or nuts as snacks. Teaching full-time while managing this, while each kid has Zoom school at top volume in a different room, so sonically, you bounce all day from a seventh-grade Zoom hellscape to a second-grade one. Sometimes you're in both at once. All that noise, their loud voices warping the sound from the laptop speakers. When you look over your younger son's shoulder, you see all the seven-year-olds wiggling in their boxes like some kind of deranged aquarium. It makes you seasick. The children like school but hate online school, complain about it and bicker all day. You try patiently to refute their arguments while also working full time, feeding them every meal and a hundred snacks, keeping abreast of the filthy disaster your house has become with four people living in it ceaselessly and without respite for months on end. You do this for an entire school year in which they fail tests and, in the older child's case, whole classes, yet somehow manage to progress to their next grades. You adults, and later the older child, manage to get vaccinated.

In the summer of 2021 there's camp, though it has to be 100% outdoors because the plague still prevails. No camp when it rains, which is often in Northeast Ohio. In most summers you could absorb the days off by giving up your own writing, but now you're both teaching full-time because the pandemic has reshaped the college's academic year.

Then straight from the teaching summer into the teaching fall, when you've had no time to prepare and no break from teaching or parenting or really from anything—and still not even a single full-night's uninterrupted sleep—in eighteen straight months.

MOTHERS UNEARTHED

All of this happens fundamentally because global climate change displaces animals from their habitats and brings them into contact with new environments and species. Novel viruses like H1N1 and SARS-COV-2 introduce themselves into human populations. And human populations have different ideas about science, about the spread of disease, about societal responsibility. More aggressive public health measures in March 2020 could have saved hundreds of thousands of lives, put children back in school, lessened all manner of suffering. So yes, you are boiling over with rage.

* * *

Hundreds of thousands of people are dead, and still many refuse to mask. It curtails their freedom. They don't claim it curtails their freedom to need a driver's license, or to pay taxes to resurface local roads. They won't get vaccinated because they live in a world in which scientists lie, have ulterior motives, want to make people infertile, magnetic; want to commit genocide. (Sometimes, as the Shoah teaches us, scientists do work in the service of genocide; but thus far vaccines seem to improve public health rather than murder people.)

Ohio driver's licenses expire on your birthday, so in September 2021 I go to the BMV to get mine renewed. BMV is what people call the DMV here in Ohio, where people are either humorless or mature enough not to laugh about the first two letters being BM. Aside from one employee, I am the only person wearing a mask. White people in their 20s, white people in their 80s. Polite, waiting calmly in line, filling out forms and answering required questions, not talking loudly on their phones or complaining or sniping at the workers' speed as folks tend to do back in New Jersey; all seemingly certain that this public health disaster that we're in the midst of is behind us. Maybe none of them have unvaccinated children at home, or vaccinated elderly parents they want to spare from breakthrough infections, or neighbors with weak immune systems. I focus on other people when the mask is uncomfortable; I remind myself why it's important to wear it. Not that I want to catch this disease, either. A mild case still sounds terrible, and my mother died of a freak respiratory illness at exactly my age. This can happen to anyone, and in my heart I irrationally believe it will happen to me. If anything happens to my unvaccinated son, I'll blame myself forever. Do these mild-mannered white people have anyone about whom they feel the same way? Do they also consider it an expression of their freedom to buy a car as big as they want, to generate as much trash as they please, to water their lawn to verdant greenness, to play golf on a golf course that uses up a whole neighborhood's worth of water?

Controlling the virus and reversing climate change both mean recalibrating what's necessary. We don't need to have complete freedom of choice about what cars we drive, but we do need to stop extracting fossil fuels. All of us need to mask to ensure freedom of movement for people with more fragile immune systems. But that's an assault on freedom, say the gentle, maskless faces of the people in the BMV, even though what they mean is that it curbs their license to do as they please—that license itself a fiction, a societal dream, a historical anomaly no one but an oligarch would ever have considered their due before now.

* * *

Americans discount global climate change because until recently, the consequences happened far away. Perhaps it's as difficult to imagine the scale of the loss when much of Southeast Asia is leveled by a tsunami as for some non-Jews to believe 6,000,000 of us were murdered in the Shoah. Where is the evidence? Who knew them? (We did. We were them, they were our families.)

Now climate disaster creeps closer. California wildfires, New York and New Jersey and Western Europe leveled by floods. Lots of people discount the Midwest—one colleague disparages those "who consider it a *mortal wound* to live in a fly-over state"—but right now, Northeast Ohio is a pretty safe bet, when you think about sea-level rise. It seems— as did my childhood home—like a place where that could never happen.

* * *

I wish I thought our geographical location meant our children were safe. In the short term, they likely won't become climate refugees, though we've been joking for years that as adults, they'll be foraging in the jungles of Canada. Also, it's not a joke. Also, we're Jews, so we keep our passports and cash handy in case we need to cross the border. If we and our children don't have to flee pogroms or climate disaster, does that mean we'll be taking in refugees, or, God forbid, turning them away? Is it possible more will come than we can take? Do we need to start harvesting acorns? Planting hazelnuts and pawpaw? Growing potatoes where now our children run with the dog in the grass?

* * *

Am I paranoid? So many times, non-Jewish, non-female friends have asked if I was blowing things out of proportion when I experienced anti-Semitism and misogyny. The doctor I've stopped seeing prescribes my husband sleeping pills to help him cope with our younger son's constant assault on our sleep. She refuses to offer any to me. "Obviously your son needs you; it would be dangerous to take anything." And when I express concern about sudden weight gain: "Have you heard of exercise? Exercise is widely believed to help people lose weight." A woman doctor practices this way in the twenty-first century? Your department chair really said that about Yom Kippur? Are you sure you're not exaggerating? Yes.

* * *

"School mask mandates violate my parental freedoms," but your unmasked child violates the social contract.

* * *

As the children grow, my rage toward them wanes. They still overtouch but don't use me, as a friend recently said of her toddler, as their "personal jungle gym." They eat a wider variety of foods, throw fewer tantrums, begin employing reason more often than a loud, crazed simulacrum of reason. ("Don't be a Trumpy," the little one says to the big one about his bombast, and I think, oh God, is that where they learned how to bluster and storm?) The rage doesn't disappear. It remains the base state. But it diverts. There are more worthy targets.

* * *

A paranoid delusion typically harms only the paranoid. Unless he's a young, white, American man. He can stockpile military-grade weapons and go shoot up a school, a synagogue, a mosque, a Hindu temple, a black church, a supermarket, a massage parlor, a movie theater, an Independence Day parade. He can murder children, women, grandparents, immigrants, black people, anyone whose religious beliefs differ from his own—any kind of person he feels has wronged him. In which case there's nothing we can do as a society due to the Second Amendment, say the originalists. Assault weapons are nothing the Founding Fathers could have imagined. In 1791, when they ratified the Amendment, rifles weren't even in common use; a musket ball often missed its target, and the weapon took a minute to load. And the Amendment clearly describes a "well regulated Militia," emphasis on the "well regulated," and does not describe proto-military loner wingnuts.

Shortly after the massacre at Sandy Hook Elementary, I got pregnant with my second child, and could envision another horrible possible end for both my children. Ten years later, when a similar massacre takes place in Uvalde, TX, our government is still wringing its hands. There is nothing well-regulated about murdering children. Our society condones paranoias that kill people, such as guns and resistance to vaccines. Everything else is *paranoia* paranoia. This despite the fact that so many of us believe climate scientists and epidemiologists and common sense, that we get ourselves and our eligible children vaccinated, that we want to keep weapons designed only to kill and maim people out of the hands of everyday civilians, that we want our world to make it.

* * *

If you can afford it, you can buy a plug-in electric or hybrid car, bike or walk to work. You can shut off every light in your house when not using it, install low-energy bulbs, turn down the thermostat at night, teach your children not to flush the toilet every time they pee, though if you do this, you may regret it. You can shop at your local store instead of online. You can buy local, organic produce—again, if you can afford it—or grow it if you have a plot of land and time and expertise or a willingness to learn. You can forage. You can leave chemicals off your lawn and harvest the dandelion greens. You can feed your kids a diet of actual, recognizable foods, if you don't live in a food desert and have time to prepare meals. This is a lot of ifs, mostly class-based. And these measures make little difference without systemic change, which again and again, in way after way, those white people in line at the BMV show us holds no interest.

* * *

When I was dating, it seemed like someone was always breaking up with me, giving up instead of trying to fix something. Maybe this was inevitable, because the few times I broke up with men, they hounded and cajoled. One came so unhinged that my landlady and I had the locks on the house changed. If there was a problem, men would say, "This isn't working, it's over," rather than working through it. With every breakup, I felt hurt that the person who says no always seems to win. Optimists and the willing get left behind.

* * *

Some of us are not only willing to make change but recognize it as the only route to survival. For most it's too much trouble, too freedom-curtailing. Liberty, license. But I don't see how they can break up with the rest of humanity. They're stuck with us as surely as we're stuck with them.

* * *

My neighbor—the brilliant artist with whom I trade perfumes— is working with NASA to design a spaceship expected to launch to

Proxima B in 2069. I'll be a hundred years old; more likely dead. I wish I could see the spaceship; wish I could be here if our species ever meets one from another planet. My sons have, God willing, a good chance of living to see that spaceship blast off toward that unimaginable distance, if civilization holds. They'll be two of the billions of people carrying civilization forward. They like science, they're adept at math, they read voraciously, they believe in the Jewish values of *tzedakah v'chesed*, charity and lovingkindness. I hope this means they're equipped to learn what they'll need to adapt and invent. Maybe the future needs someone who can blow a trombone.

* * *

In the news: Vaccinated people, who trust science, line up for booster shots when eligible. Vaccine skeptics say the booster represents clear evidence the vaccines don't work. Our unvaccinated coworker's opinion doesn't change no matter what information we share with her. Her pastor told her mRNA vaccines kill laboratory animals. He cites a source for this news; by my standards it's not a credible source, but she holds her own opinion. She feels that in the same way she respects our choices even when she disagrees with them (for example on the subject of childrearing), we should respect hers.

The difference, I try to explain, is that what goes on in a colleague's apparently peaceful home in no way affects her, while her ignoring a public health directive can kill her or any of us. She tells me that we are not always as open-minded as we claim to be; and I know there are senses in which she's right. Our institution's head of pandemic protocols says we must respect her views. Why, I ask, when they're unfounded? We don't have to respect the views, she amends, we have to respect her right to hold them. We have to respect her. And we do. Our respect for her is one of the many reasons we want to keep her safe. The institution has, however, taken no action against those who violate its vaccine mandate. If it isn't enforced, it's not a mandate. People who don't want to protect themselves, their coworkers, and their coworkers' families from a scourge of an illness are allowed to say no, to break up with the social contract. This does not all fit under the heading of respect.

* * *

Another academic year ends, and thus far all of us in this office, and those we care for, have made it through. *Shehechiyanu*, says the Jewish prayer for when something memorable and new occurs, or when the year cycles around to a holiday or observance: "Thank you for keeping us alive, sustaining us, and allowing us to reach this season."

One colleague caught the virus, still feels unwell months later. A friend who recently recovered suffered a pulmonary embolism—a common outcome for Covid survivors on birth control. We all wear masks in the office and the classroom, as well as in Target and at the library and the post office. The children in this office pod who were too young to be vaccinated at the start of the school year are vaccinated now. Our colleague's elderly parents remain alive, if frailer.

Shehechiyanu. Thank you for letting us continue our work for as long as we can do that, as long as we can live given this pandemic, given the increasing velocity of climate change, given our overall lack of respect for each other and this planet.

* * *

The rage I have felt about every instance of misogyny, anti-Semitism, unfairness—my own, out in the world—dims in comparison to this rage, which burns white hot day and night. People can't be allowed to say no to their fellow humans, or to the future itself, without immediate consequences. The long-term consequences are coming for us all. Maybe mother-rage will drive change, or maybe it will do what I suspect it has always done, immolate women, burn us up from the inside. I can't square this with my own desire to work, live, make art, rest, be a person in this world, and raise my children as part of that. If I cast my mind forward into the future I won't live to see, I can at least imagine the spaceship, my kids and my neighbor's kids watching it launch, remembering their mothers as they do their small part of *tikkun olam*, repairing the world.

We Were Warned

Belle Boggs

I remember every moment of my mother's fury—rare, but terrifying—when she felt that her children were threatened. My mother was five foot zero, a hundred pounds, and usually dressed in paint-spattered shortalls. But, she could become large, loud, and scary to protect us. On the phone with the greedy insurance company that refused to cover my brother's asthma treatments, at a meeting with the sexist principal who didn't believe me when I said I'd been assaulted, on a floating dock in the Mattaponi River where an old man threatened us with a gun—she transformed into a hippie goddess of rage.

By the time I had my daughters, Beatrice and Harriet, I was more than a decade older than my mother was when she had me. You could say I was more mellow at 37 than my mother had been at 25. I've spent less time arguing with insurance companies and writing checks to "Shittybank" (which, she always pointed out, they cashed). My one gun-carrying neighbor is a friend of mine who mows the banks of the river spot where my girls and I play. Plus, I take an antidepressant. That helps, too.

For a while I thought my husband and I might never have children—not because we didn't want them, but because we were infertile and unsure how far to go with treatments. Maybe it was more responsible not to have children at all, I sometimes thought. Would it be better for the earth to direct those resources elsewhere? Now, less than a decade later, I know that I was asking the wrong questions.

What terrifies and fills me with anguish is not what the earth endures, because of the carbon footprints planted by my seven-year-old and three-year-old, but what my daughters, and every other child alive today, will endure in their lifetimes on earth. I am afraid, especially because I was older when I had them, that I won't be there to protect them, to the extent that I *could* protect them from threats that feel far beyond my control. I'm afraid that they will confront the mess that my generation and my parents' generation and the one before has left them. They'll face all of it—water scarcity, war, heat waves, unimaginable storms—alone, without even the balm of their own progeny.

I say this to you, because I cannot say it to them: I do not believe that we will solve the climate crisis before it becomes insurmountable. I don't believe it in the same way that I don't believe in God: with sorrow that I can't believe, with hope that I might be wrong, and with growing, furious certainty that I am not. I am so angry, and so sorry, and so fearful for them.

* * *

Even in my rural, underfunded, 1980s elementary-middle school, we learned about the greenhouse effect: how fossil fuels were clogging the atmosphere with carbon dioxide, which trapped and reflected heat back to the earth's surface. This must have been around 1988, when the director of NASA's Institute for Space Studies testified before Congress that "the greenhouse effect has been detected, and it is changing our climate now." We learned this as a fact documented by science rather than as a political, debatable opinion.

I remember thinking, even then, that the greenhouse effect sounded harder to fix than phosphate-caused algae blooms or the DDT poisoning of bald eagles, the other environmental issues I'd learned about through school and science fair projects—maybe even impossible. But I worried more about my own path: out of the poor, conservative place where I lived, which my father (a realist, if also a hippie) had warned me would be developed beyond recognition by the time I grew up. I loved our home near the river, but I accepted what my dad told me. Plus, I wanted to be a writer. The county where we lived had no bookstores, nowhere to see a play or a movie, not even a public library.

I'm not sure who I thought would solve the problem of the climate crisis, or when I thought it would happen. It wasn't a crisis, then—at least, it felt like a far-away crisis, not the number-one task of every human alive today, which is how it feels now. The ponds and lakes around our house still froze solid enough for ice skating; even our wide, tidal river froze. We had many snow days, and only one hurricane day that I remember. Thunderstorms were pleasant. If you'd asked me then, will you have children, and will your children have children, I would have said, *Of course! I'll have two children, just like my parents, and they can do whatever they like. And, yes, they will have children.*

* * *

"We need clean water for our children, and our children's children," said the governor of my state at the university where I taught in fall of 2021, when EPA administrator Michael Regan announced a plan for combating per- and polyfluoroalkyl substances, or PFAS.

These are the dangerous, largely unregulated "forever chemicals" dumped into our waterways—and those across the country—by chemical companies like Dupont and Chemours, which sell them to other companies making non-stick, stain-resistant, and flame-retardant goods. PFAS take thousands of years to degrade. Beatrice and I swim in a river that's full of them, we know this because it's also our town's closest source of drinking water. "Don't put your head under the water," I remind Bea every time we swim. When she ignores me, I plead: "Don't open your mouth. Don't open your eyes."

PFAS, which are toxic and carcinogenic, are in Teflon coatings and water-repellent fabrics, in furniture and car seats, in drinking water and in the blood and urine of most Americans, including children. Roy Cooper, our governor in North Carolina, is a good leader, and Michael Regan, the first Black man to lead the EPA, is even better, having worked for years to combat PFAS and climate injustice. But when Cooper said, "our children's children," I thought he probably meant his children, who are adults, and not my children or Michael Regan's child, all under ten years old. It's hard for me to believe young children will have much choice in how their lives will go, which includes planning for their families. They won't even be old enough to vote in 2030—the time by which most scientists agree we need to have halted climate change to avoid the worst consequences. The worst meaning: mass extinction; disastrous flooding, storms, and wildfires; famine; large parts of the world rendered uninhabitable.

And meanwhile, shortly after the announcement that poison-producers would be held accountable, North Carolina's Department of Health and Human Services decided not to change the acceptable PFAS levels in our drinking water—currently far above what the EPA considers safe. An easy fix! Just... don't dump them anymore. Better yet, don't produce them at all. Who needs nonstick cookware? Or water and stain-repellent fabric? It's not like those things are one hundred percent necessary—like water.

We'd wait, North Carolina said, until the EPA finished its evaluation of the known toxin that has produced some of the worst-quality drinking water in the entire country.

We won't solve the climate crisis. Not in time for *our children, and our children's children*. It's too easy to say we'll wait, we'll study it, we'll do that later. *Blah blah blah*, as Greta Thunberg said at the 2021 Youth4Climate Summit in Milan. At the end of that speech, she said that she still has hope, but does she, truly?

"You have stolen my dreams, and my childhood, with your empty words," Thunberg told the United Nations in 2019. This feels completely true, and utterly damning. I watched the short speech on YouTube with Beatrice, who replayed it immediately. "Blah blah blah," she repeated, echoing Greta's defiance, enjoying the spectacle of a hoodie-wearing young person speaking back, with unapologetic anger, to a large room of suit-wearing adults.

* * *

Another reason I don't believe we'll make enough changes necessary to mitigate the climate crisis? Our country's terrible, politicized mishandling of the pandemic, which at this writing has killed nearly one million Americans. Most adults have had vaccine eligibility for almost a year, yet because of the same political manipulation that divides us about climate change, fifteen percent of American adults remain unvaccinated. This despite the fact that vaccines are life-saving, protective of the whole community.

I direct a lot of the anger I feel about the climate crisis toward our lax pandemic safety measures and how we prioritize money over the lives of children. In gerrymandered-to-hell states like mine, the pandemic has been a useful stand-in for other issues of justice, health, and adherence to science—a kind of test case for our ability to make informed choices and address bigger problems. I have lost my mind in grocery stores and PTA meetings and my own workplace over how badly we're failing at the relatively easy task of protecting people against a deadly disease, how afraid we are of offending the Covid-deniers and vaccine-resisters and people who just prefer not to wear a mask.

The university where I teach, where our governor and EPA administrator came to speak, does not require that our students get vaccinated against Covid. This is a political calculation, an attempt to shield our institution from the wrath of a Republican legislature that doesn't give two slaps about higher education, lower education, kids, animals, plants, air, water, or old people who don't vote Republican. "The good news is, you can get vaccinated," faculty and staff are told regularly, when we point out that a vaccine mandate is entirely legal, protective of the whole community, and—especially—protective for the young children that many of us go home to.

Last fall, one of my students worked nights as an EMT in a local emergency room. He had to have violence prevention training to protect himself from Covid patients who demand the vaccine when it's too late, when they're about to be intubated. He came to school exhausted, his eyes shadowed by dark circles that contrasted with his stark white K-N95 mask.

And do young people come in with Covid? I asked him once, selfishly thinking of my own kids and hoping he'd say no.

The saddest patients are the babies, he said.

* * *

In the first summer of the pandemic, a beloved member of the writing community where I live died suddenly and unexpectedly. I spoke to a friend and colleague not long after, and he shared that, in addition to the sorrow he felt at the loss of his friend, he was afraid. What if he died before this book that he was working on now was finished? He had other books to write, too—other things to say. Did I worry about the books I'd leave unwritten, if I died suddenly?

My friend does not have children, and our friend who died did not have kids either. I didn't say to him that unfinished books were the least of my worries, not even in the top ten of my fears, because I hated, before I had kids, when people with children suggested that they existed on a separate, more important plane from the rest of us. More serious, more fraught, with bigger things to worry about. They were right, it turns out; at least, that's how I see things now.

A couple of months after my friend and I spoke about unfinished books, I took Beatrice, then six years old, with me to an all-ages, get-out-the vote march in Alamance County, North Carolina, where I'd been reporting on the Black Lives Matter movement. I went to this march not as a reporter, but as a mom. I wanted my daughter to see the power of voting and community. I wanted her to experience marching side by side with other citizens who believed, as we do, that all people have the right to make their voices heard.

MOTHERS UNEARTHED

Less than thirty minutes into the march, just after we finished kneeling in the street in remembrance of George Floyd, police pepper-fogged us and about 200 other protesters, many of them kids. As we stumbled away. If I had been my own mother, I would have been in jail. I would have leapt upon the police, who didn't even help the children choking and coughing and screaming, who didn't offer us water. I didn't yell. I clutched my daughter, hoisted her onto my back. Another protester gave us water to rinse our eyes and mouths, which stung long afterwards.

The scenario would be a good novel opener, my friend who worried about dying with an unfinished novel later told me.. A novel! The mother's guilt over not protecting her child—who might, in the novel, suffer a worse fate than Beatrice had experienced—would make for propulsive action, he suggested.

No white child's experience should be centered in that kind of story, I told him. Cops willing to pepper-fog children, disabled and elderly people. Cops eager to arrest Black people on their way to vote. The truth was bad enough.

I said nothing to my friend about my guilt. My guilt is a well—unseen, but deep, connected to the coursing aquifers of my anger and fear.

The climate crisis is here, is growing worse, and I'm afraid we'll face it like Covid deniers facing intubation: with chaos and violence and remorse that we didn't see it coming, even though we did. Even though we were warned.

I'm angry just about every day—like my mom and like my daughters will be, whether they become mothers or not. My children, and yours, will have the right to be furious with every one of us who didn't heed the warnings, the older folks who will leave them alone with rising seas and terrible storms, with not enough water, food, or hope. They will know, with certainty, that it won't be getting better, only worse.

And yet, my daughters, like I was, are surrounded by love and nature; they are having a happy childhood that is also, I hope, preparing them for the years ahead. We swim in the Haw River, pick up trash along its banks, grow mudpuddle-stranded tadpoles in Mason jars on our porch. The tadpoles, the green riverbanks, even the small kindnesses extended to Beatrice after the march when we were pepper-fogged are growing, in my daughters, the capacity for bravery and amazement at the life around us, even as they see that it's under constant attack. Fostering this growth, this amazement, and this courage is the most important work I do.

Recently I was given a high price quote on a term life insurance policy. "But I'm a vegetarian!" I insisted to our mild-mannered financial advisor. "My blood pressure is perfect!"

"It's the history of anxiety," he said gently. "And the medication you take? The antidepressant?" He tried to explain how, in an actuarial sense, this made me a bigger risk.

"Everyone I know, other than you, has anxiety," I snapped. He calmly repeated the part about actuarial tables, and we settled on a lower level of coverage.

"I can't die anyway," I said, my anger dissipating just a little as I realized this complicated, impossible truth. "My kids need me."

Contributor Bios & Acknowedgments

Kianny N. Antigua. Fiction writer, poet and translator. She is a Senior Lecturer of Spanish at Dartmouth College, and an independent translator and adapter for Pepsqually VO Sound & Design, Inc. Antigua has published twenty-three books of children's literature, five of short stories, two collections of poems, an anthology, a book of microfiction, a novel and a journal. She has won sixteen literary awards and many of her texts have been included in anthologies, literary magazines, newspapers and textbooks. Some have been translated into English, French and Italian. She is the translator (Eng./Spa.) and the audiobook narrator of *Dominicana* (Seven Stories Press, 2021), by Angie Cruz; translator of *Mi buena mala suerte*, by Ruth Behar; and the YA novel *Nunca mires atrás* (Bloomsbury/Audible, 2022), by Lilliam Rivera.

Emily Barton is the author of three novels: *The Book of Esther*, *Brookland*, and *The Testament of Yves Gundron*. Her fiction, criticism, and essays have appeared in many publications; she writes most often for *The New York Times Book Review*. Her work has been recognized with grants and fellowships from the Guggenheim Foundation, the National Endowment for the Arts, the Corporation of Yaddo, and the Sustainable Arts Foundation. Barton has also won the Bard Fiction Prize. She has taught, among other places, at New York University, Yale University, Columbia University, and Smith College, and currently chairs the creative writing program at Oberlin College.

Belle Boggs is the author of *The Gulf: A Novel*; *The Art of Waiting*; and *Mattaponi Queen: Stories*. *The Art of Waiting* was a finalist for the PEN/Diamonstein-Spielvogel Award for the Art of the Essay and was named a best book of the year by *Kirkus*, *Publishers Weekly*, the *Globe and Mail*, *Buzzfeed*, and *O, the Oprah Magazine*. *Mattaponi Queen*, a collection of linked stories set along Virginia's Mattaponi River, won the Bakeless Prize and the Library of Virginia Literary Award and was a finalist for the 2010 Frank O'Connor International Short Story Award. She has received fellowships from the National Endowment for the Arts, the North Carolina Arts Council, and the Bread Loaf and Sewanee writers' conferences. Her stories and essays have appeared in the *Atlantic Monthly*, *Orion*, the *Paris Review*, *Harper's*, *Ecotone*, *Ploughshares*, and elsewhere. She is professor of English at North Carolina State University, where she also directs the MFA program in creative writing.

Claire Boyles (she/her) is a writer and a former farmer. A 2022 Whiting Award winner in fiction, she is the author of *Site Fidelity*, which was longlisted for the PEN/Robert W. Bingham Award and is a finalist for the Reading the West Award for Debut Fiction and the Colorado Book Award. Her writing has appeared in *VQR*, *Kenyon Review*, *Boulevard*, and *Masters Review*, among others. She is a Peter Taylor Fellow for the Kenyon Review Writing Workshops and has received support from the Kimmel Harding Nelson Foundation, the Bread Loaf Orion Environmental Writers Workshop, and the Community of Writers. She teaches in Eastern Oregon University's low-residency MFA program in Creative and Environmental Writing.

Sujatha Fernandes is a writer, scholar, and teacher. She is a Professor of Sociology at the University of Sydney, where she founded the Racial

Justice and the Curriculum Project. Her short stories have appeared in *New Ohio Review, Saranac Review, Aster(ix)*, and *The Maine Review*. Her essays have been published in the *New York Times, The Nation*, and forthcoming in *Orion Magazine*. She is the author of a memoir on a global hip hop life *Close to the Edge* (Verso), a collection of essays *The Cuban Hustle* (Duke University Press), and *Curated Stories: The Uses and Misuses of Storytelling* (Oxford). She is an editorial board member of the literary magazine *Transition: The Magazine of Africa and the Diaspora* and edited a special issue with Jared Thomas on Bla(c)kness in Australia. She is currently completing a collection of interlinked short stories *Shadow People*, and a novel *Beyond the Monsoon Mountains*.

Carolyn Ferrell is the author of *Dear Miss Metropolitan*, which was recently shortlisted for both the PEN Hemingway Award for Debut Novel and the PEN Faulkner Award for Fiction. Her first book, a short-story collection *Don't Erase Me*, was awarded the 1997 Art Seidenbaum Award for First Fiction of the *Los Angeles Times* Book Prize, the John C. Zacharis First Book Award given by *Ploughshares*, and the Quality Paperback Book Prize for First Fiction. Ferrell's stories and essays have been anthologized in *The Best American Short Stories* 2020 and 2018, edited by Curtis Sittenfeld and Roxane Gay, respectively; *The Best American Short Stories of the Century*, edited by John Updike; *Children of the Night: The Best Short Stories by Black Writers, 1967 to the Present*, edited by Gloria Naylor; *Apple, Tree: Writers on Their Parents*, edited by Lise Funderburg; and other places. She is the recipient of grants and awards from the Fulbright Association, the German Academic Exchange Service (DAAD), the Bronx Council on the Arts, the National Endowment for the Arts, and Sarah Lawrence College. Since 1996, she has been a faculty member in both the undergraduate and MFA writing programs at Sarah Lawrence College. She lives in New York.

MOTHERS UNEARTHED

January Gill O'Neil is an associate professor at Salem State University, and the author of *Rewilding* (2018), *Misery Islands* (2014), and *Underlife* (2009), all published by CavanKerry Press. From 2012-2018, she served as the executive director of the Massachusetts Poetry Festival, and currently serves on the boards of AWP and Montserrat College of Art. Her poems and articles have appeared in *The New York Times Magazine*, the Academy of American Poets' *Poem-A-Day* series, *American Poetry Review*, *Green Mountains Review*, *Poetry*, and *Sierra magazine*, among others. The recipient of fellowships from the Massachusetts Cultural Council, Cave Canem, and the Barbara Deming Memorial Fund, O'Neil was the 2019-2020 John and Renée Grisham Writer-in-Residence at the University of Mississippi, Oxford. She lives with her two children in Beverly, MA.

Nimmi Gowrinathan is a Tamil Sri-Lankan activist-scholar. She is a Professor at the City College of New York, where she founded the Politics of Sexual Violence Initiative, a global initiative that draws on in-depth research to inform movement-building around the impact of sexual violence on women's political identities. As a key part of this initiative she created Beyond Identity: A Gendered Platform for Scholar-Activists, a program that seeks to train immigrants and students of color in identity-driven research, political writing, and activism anchored in a thoughtful analysis of structural violence. She provides expert analysis for CNN, MSNBC, AL Jazeera, and the BBC and her writing on gender and violence has been published in *Harper's Magazine, Freeman's Journal, Foreign Affairs*, and *Guernica Magazine* among others. She is the creator of the Female Fighter Series at *Guernica Magazine* and the Publisher of *Adi Magazine*, a new literary journal to rehumanize policy. Her recent book, *Radicalizing Her*, examines the complex politics of the female fighter (Beacon 2021).

Vanessa Mártir is a 1980s Bushwick-raised bocona learning the heartbeat of silence in the countryside of upstate NY; an oil-and-water combination of ambition, imposter syndrome, procrastination, certainty, insecurity and drive. Vanessa's heart genre is creative nonfiction, & she's also a novelist, wanna be poet & playwright. She has been widely published, including in *The NY Times*, *The Washington Post*, *Longreads*, *The Guardian*, *The Rumpus*, *Bitch Magazine*, and the *NYTimes* Bestseller *Not That Bad*, edited by Roxane Gay. She is the recipient of the 2021 Letras Boricuas Fellowship, funded by The Andrew W. Mellon Foundation and the Flamboyan Foundation's Arts Fund; a 2019 Bronx Recognizes Its Own (BRIO) Award in Creative Nonfiction; a 2019 AWP Kurt Brown Award in Creative Nonfiction; and a 2013 Jerome Foundation Award. Vanessa is the creator of the Writing Our Lives Workshop and the Writing the Mother Wound movement. She has partnered with Tin House and The Rumpus to publish WOL alumni, and with Longreads and NYU's Latinx Project to publish Mother Wound essays. She has also served as guest editor of *Aster(ix)* and *The James Franco Review*. When she's not writing or teaching, you can find Vanessa in an old growth forest, listening to the birds and talking to the trees.

Marie Myung-Ok Lee is an acclaimed Korean-American writer and author of the novel *Somebody's Daughter*. Her recently published novel, *The Evening Hero*, on the future of medicine, immigration, North Korea was featured on Oprah and Real Simple Best of 2022 lists. She graduated from Brown University and was a Writer in Residence there before she began teaching at Columbia University's Writing Division. Her stories and essays have been published in *The Atlantic*, T*he New York Times*, *Slate*, *Salon*, *Guernica*, and *The Guardian*, among others. She was the first Fulbright Scholar to Korea in creative writing and has received many honors for her work, including an O. Henry honorable mention, the Best Book Award from the Friends of American Writers, and a Rhode Island State Council on the Arts fiction fellowship and is a current New York Foundation for the Arts Fiction Fellow. She has been a Yaddo and MacDowell Colony fellow and has served as a judge for the National Book Award and the PEN/E.O. Wilson Literary Science Writing Award. In addition, Ms. Lee is a founder of the Asian American Writers' Workshop and was an Our Word Writer in Residence for the Columbia MFA program.

Stacy Parker Le Melle is the author of *Government Girl: Young and Female in the White House* (HarperCollins/Ecco) and was the lead contributor to *Voices from the Storm: The People of New Orleans on Hurricane Katrina and Its Aftermath* (McSweeney's). She chronicles stories for The Katrina Experience: An Oral History Project. Her essay "Ferry Cross the Mersey" was selected for publication as one of the winners of the 2021 Thornwillow Patrons' Prize. She currently serves as Executive Editor for W.K.Kellogg Foundation's Solidarity Council on Racial Equity. In 2020, she was named a NYSCA/NYFA Artist Fellow for Nonfiction Literature. Her recent narrative nonfiction has been recently published in *Nat. Brut, The Offing, Phoebe, Silk Road* among other publications. She co-founded and curates Harlem's First Person Plural Reading Series.

Deesha Philyaw's debut short story collection, *The Secret Lives of Church Ladies,* won the 2021 PEN/Faulkner Award for Fiction, the 2020/2021 Story Prize, and the 2020 *LA Times* Book Prize: The Art Seidenbaum Award for First Fiction and was a finalist for the National Book Award for Fiction. *The Secret Lives of Church Ladies* focuses on Black women, sex, and the Black church, and is being adapted for television by HBO Max with Tessa Thompson executive producing. Deesha will be the 2022-2023 John and Renée Grisham Writer-in-Residence at the

University of Mississippi.

Chika Unigwe is the author of *Night Dancer, On Black Sisters' Street* (Random House), and *Better Never Than Late* (Cassava Republic). Her work has been translated into several languages (including French and German) and won the 2012 Nigeria Prize for Literature. Her stories and essays have appeared in *The Guardian, The New York Times,* Al Jazeera, *Guernica, The Kenyon Review, Agni,* and *Mslexia.* Born in Enugu, Nigeria,Unigwe is a professor of writing at Georgia College and State University, Milledgeville, where she sits on the MFA faculty, and is a guest lecturer at Erasmus Hoge School, Brussels. She writes a regular column for *Daily Trust Nigeria* and contributes often as a guest columnist to *MO* Belgium.* She divides her time between Milledgeville and Atlanta where she lives with her family. Her new novel will be out in the US and UK in 2023.

Acknowledgments

Parts of Printiss Polk's interview in "Prime Coats" by Stacy Parker Le Melle was published online at *The Huffington Post* in 2006.